STONE

designing kitchens,
baths, and interiors
with natural stone

HEATHER & EARL G. ADAMS, JR.

Stewart, Tabori & Chang
New York

Published in 2003 by
Stewart, Tabori & Chang
A Company of La Martinière Groupe
115 West 18th Street
New York, NY 10011

Export Sales to all countries except Canada, France, and French-speaking Switzerland:
Thames and Hudson Ltd.
181A High Holborn
London WC1V 7QX
England

Canadian Distribution:
Canadian Manda Group
One Atlantic Avenue, Suite 105
Toronto, Ontario M6K 3E7
Canada

Library of Congress Cataloging-in-Publication Data
Adams, Heather E.
  Stone : designing kitchens, bath & interiors with natural stone / by Heather E. Adams and Earl G. Adams, Jr.
    p.cm.
  Includes Index
  ISBN 1-58479-290-6
  1. Stone in interior decoration.. I. Adams, Earl G. II. Title.

NK2115.5.S76A33 2003
728—dc21

                        2002044665

The text of this book was composed in Granjon and Helvetica Neue.
Edited by Marisa Bulzone and Trudi Bartow
Designed by Allyson McFarlane
Graphic Production by Kim Tyner

Printed in China
10 9 8 7 6 5 4 3 2 1

First Printing

DEDICATION

We would like to dedicate this book to our family and friends, our two little boys, Reese and Rion, and especially Carla and Dale Steinbach for their enormous support, advice, and creative words.

ACKNOWLEDGMENTS

First and foremost, we must thank our family and friends for their unwavering support and for mirroring our enthusiasm for the book. Your help will never be forgotten. Thank you to our precious little boys, Reese and Rion, for being so incredibly patient as we worked from dawn until late into the night. Thank you to the talented architects, builders, designers, tradesmen, and homeowners whose visions helped to create the images gracing the pages of *Stone*. We can not overlook the skilled photographers whose eyes for composition and lighting capture the true essence of these lovely spaces on film.

Next, this book would not exist if it were not for our wonderful agent, Stephany Evans, our editors, Marisa Bulzone and Trudi Bartow, and our designer, Allyson McFarlane. They too were infected with our enthusiasm and love for natural stone and chose to take on the project. We cannot thank you enough.

We must also extend our gratitude to the following individuals for their help in gathering the perfect photos to tell the story of stone. In no particular order we would like to thank Suzie Tatum of Ann Sacks, Jonathan Zanger, Jennifer Capasso and Jenny Tsai of Walker Zanger, Ted Lowitz of Lowitz and Company, Thierry Francois of Stone Age Designs, Marty Fahey of Materials Marketing, Joy Burch of Marc-Michaels Interior Design, Jenny Hildreth of Arc PR, Gianni Casiraghi of Downsview Kitchens, Patricia Wyche of London Bay Homes, Lisa Gray and Laura Wilson of Sonoma Tile Makers, Katherine Kagler of Architerra, Philip Smith of Akdo Intertrade, Mark Schmidt of Studio Vertu, Erica Remuzzi of Oceanside Glasstile, Lisa McDaniel of Benning Design, Myrna Gustafson of de Giulio Kitchen Design, Amy Riggs of Mesa Precast, Victoria Murray and Jodi Dawson of Country Floors Australia, Mary Mac Stukes of Rutt of Atlanta, Desmond Keogh of Hafia Inc., Mikal Otten of William Ohs Custom Cabinetry, Andrea Thomas and Lori Carroll of Lori Carroll and Associates, Liz Ryan and Jennifer Jensen of Liz Ryan Design, Caroline Hansberry of Sidnam Petrone and Gartner Architects, Rita of Granite-Tops Inc., Leah Lubin of Beateworks, Nelson Londono of Artsaics, Melissa McClure of Dal Tile, Denise Rosenstein of Barbara Tattersfield Designs, Hillary Kendrick of Image Architects, and all of the wonderful photographers' assistants; your help has been greatly appreciated. We have met so many wonderful people during the writing of *Stone*, we sincerely apologize if we did not include your name in the above list.

INTRODUCTION: THE ESSENCE OF STONE

THE ESSENCE OF STONE

Since the dawn of time, stone has left its indelible mark upon the face of the Earth. Withstanding the forces of nature as no other natural material could, indigenous rock endured the ravages of wind, water, and sand in its endeavor to persevere. From the great pyramids of Egypt to the stone giants of Easter Island, it has bowed, but never broken. You need only look around to notice what material the world's greatest masters have chosen to create their monuments or in what medium history's most renowned artisans elected to carve their works. Whether it was to build their cities or for protection, the ancients used indestructible walls of stone as their foundation. From the ancient civilizations of Peru to the Mayan ruins of Mexico, these antediluvian cities will forever remain upon the landscape as testimonials to the immortal endurance of stone. Perhaps it is this fundamental determination to persist against all odds that has been the catalyst behind our fascination, or it may be possible that somewhere, buried deep within the human psyche, exists an unwavering instinct for survival that leaves us all mesmerized by this unrelenting material. After all, early man relied on stone for nearly all of his rudimentary needs, including shelter, primitive weapons, tools, and even the ability to ignite fire. For thousands of years our ancestors used stone for basic survival, communication, artistic expression, and the building of their architectural edifices.

RIGHT: Mosaic strips of metal and tumbled stone form intersecting lines throughout this kitchen's slate floor.

Throughout the ages, stone has been used not only for its accessibility and practicality, but for its aesthetic beauty as well. The Greeks erected the marble-clad Parthenon high above Athens to pay homage to their gods and the Romans dotted the landscape with monuments of stone, from towering porticos and public bathhouses to massive fountains and intricately chiseled statuaries. As the Romanesque and Gothic periods emerged, stone became the central building blocks for imposing castles set high above medieval villages. Stone remained the prominent building material right down through the Renaissance, Baroque, and neoclassical periods. It was not until the onset of contemporary design that for the first time in history a less expensive man-made material superceded stone in popularity. With the advent of less-expensive-to-produce and easy-to-install products came the downfall of stone as the primary building block of construction. With time, it soon faded from widespread prominence to semi-obscurity, found only in public spaces and the opulent homes of the wealthy. Gone was the era of permanence and stability, and in its place emerged the age of the disposable society.

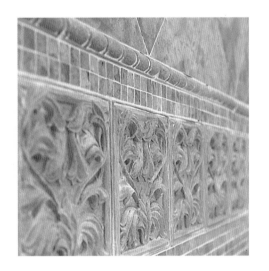  

Today we are witnessing the resurgence of natural stone within the home. Ceramic and laminate countertops are being replaced by granite and marble slabs. Floors once covered with sheets of vinyl and carpet are now graced by large-scale limestone and travertine tiles. Nondescript synthetic shower surrounds accompanied by mundane vanity tops are being tossed aside and in their place we see hand-crafted mosaics and antiquated tumbled stones. Even the exteriors of our dwellings have not been overlooked with the return of majestic stone architecture. Arches, columns, and loggias constructed of stone capture the essence of a timeworn Tuscan villa.

Once again the luxury of natural stone resurfaces within our homes thanks to the ever-changing and rapidly progressing advances in technology. These advances, combined with improved methods of quarrying, extraction, and fabrication, have all contributed to the cost reduction of natural stone products. Stone tiles and slabs, now cut thinner, are easier to package, ship, and install, and are competitively priced with most man-made materials.

If you are in the process of building or remodeling, you are most likely considering the use of natural stone somewhere in your design and it is very likely that you have been subjected to much speculation regarding its use. Much of what you have heard is presumably a combination of truth and fiction. It is the goal of this book to guide you through the selection process and familiarize you with the many facets of this timeless material. Your home should be your sanctuary, as well as meet all of your fundamental needs. In today's high-tech society, natural stone is one of the few products versatile enough to allow for the incorporation of state of the art technology, while still capturing

LEFT: Rows of handmade tile blend perfectly with the field stone and adjacent mosaic bands.

CENTER: In this bath, limestone is featured on the countertop, backsplash, and in the form of a carved bowl sink

RIGHT: Antique Dalle de Bourgogne is a stone reclaimed from old properties located in the Burgundy region of France. The stone's soft colorful patina adds authenticity to the room.

the essence of old-world charm. Stone is not only capable of adding this aura of authenticity to your home, but also ensures unsurpassed quality and immeasurable value as well. When you take into account all of these qualities, plus the fact that stone becomes more beautiful with the passage of time, you begin to wonder why anyone would consider using anything else.

For those who may harbor concerns that they will grow tired of such a permanent feature, it is important to understand the nature of the material itself. Somewhat like a chameleon, stone possesses an innate ability to change with its surroundings. After years of normal wear, a wonderful patina will surface, revealing hints of mysterious layers concealed beneath. Stone creates a solid architectural structure within the framework of the home that allows all other elements to coexist in harmony, regardless of style.

As you explore the pages ahead, you will soon discover that this book is more than just a beautiful and inspiring photo album; it also functions as a teaching aid and comprehensive resource guide. Join us as we walk you through virtually every aspect of your project. It is our sincere hope that our years of experience with natural stone products and their complementary elements will be of great assistance to you, and will help to ensure that the visions you hold in your mind's eye will someday soon become a reality. Now, let us begin our journey down the pathway of discovery, in search of the ultimate dream home, utilizing nature's most prized element—stone.

RIGHT: Escaping to a light filled master bath retreat can serve as the perfect beginning and end to each day.

THE STONE KITCHEN

TOP: Classic travertine slabs are wonderfully paired with this kitchen's playful chartreuse walls.

BOTTOM LEFT: Giallo Reale and Rojo Alicante tumbled marble merge to form a lively geometric splash design.

BOTTOM CENTER: Exotic Golden Beach granite flows over the countertop and up the splash in this modern kitchen space.

BOTTOM RIGHT: French Blue limestone found on both the counter and splash is accented by icy glass tiles.

chapter one

THE COUNTERTOP

The use of stone as a countertop material has existed for many hundreds of years. Born out of necessity in the European homes of the past, large slabs of marble and limestone served their purpose as durable and functional surfaces, lasting the lifespan of the home. Man has created many different materials since this first countertop of stone, but even today, most will agree that nature has provided us with the most beautiful and functional material for the kitchen.

Combining the kitchen and living areas in today's home has become the norm rather than the exception. No longer housed in its own individual space, the kitchen must be designed with great attention to detail. Intended to blend in wonderfully with its surroundings, the kitchen has become the convivial epicenter that must not only be functional, but beautiful as well.

Take a moment to visualize your ideal kitchen. Not everyone's vision will be the same, but natural stone usually enters the picture somewhere. When designed creatively, your kitchen can transform even the mundane task of cooking into a sensory adventure. Close your eyes. Can you smell the aroma of the warm tangy spices as they simmer on the cooktop? Do you hear the gentle hiss as a cork escapes a perfectly aged bottle of wine? When you open your eyes, what do you want to see? Is your dream kitchen one that reflects the sleek, clean lines of Asian-inspired simplicity or the old-world charm of a French country estate? Maybe you're seeking something a little more traditional or whimsical, or perhaps you yearn for the authentic look of nature with its rugged and rustic charm. Whatever your tastes, your dreams can be accomplished through the use of natural stone materials juxtaposed one against the other creating visual and tactile excitement. Whether incorporating the glasslike surface of granite, the smooth satin finish of limestone, or the rough texture of tumbled marble, you can be certain that your countertop will present a natural focal point.

With the kitchen becoming one of the most predominant living areas within the home, why not make it a feast for the senses? Even when working with a limited budget, designing a kitchen that is unique, exciting, and upscale is now more possible than ever.

Be aware that the porous surface and unfilled holes of stone countertops can collect debris during food preparation. To be safe, consider sealing or filling and use a cutting board routinely.

DIFFERENT KINDS OF STONE

Granite Pulled from the earth in giant monolithic blocks, granite is the oldest, strongest, and hardest stone available. Due to this combination of strength and beauty, granite has become one of the most highly regarded materials for countertops. Take into account its sturdiness, broad color range, and abundant options in size and finish, and you have the perfect stone for bestowing a rich elegance in

any kitchen. Granite's innate quality to stand up under the most dramatic abuse is unmatched. Whether it's in its capacity to withstand hot pots and pans placed directly upon its surface or the ability to survive as a cutting board under the assault of the sharpest of knives, you'll admire its durability and resilience. Feel free to make a mess, granite is forgiving.

Originally granite was available only in large slabs, limiting affordability to those with a sizable budget. Fortunately it has become a luxury that most homeowners can now enjoy because when budget constraints prohibit the purchase of an entire slab, scaling back to the tile

ABOVE: An innovative design statement, this lovely kitchen blends elements of both contemporary and old-world style. The long narrow island is capped with a slab of golden-hued granite.

OPPOSITE TOP: Ripples of silver and plum wash over an underlying sea of black in this exotic granite countertop aptly named Blue Wave.

OPPOSITE BOTTOM: A dash of salt and pepper granite with a subtle twist of lemon spice up this culinary corner.

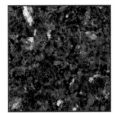

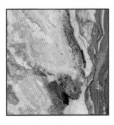

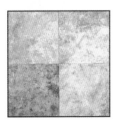

ABOVE: Examples of granite, marble, slate, travertine, and limestone. See Chapter 10 for more color choices.

format can still ensure the same look and strength at a savings of nearly 50 percent!

Proven to evoke and stimulate specific emotions, color sets the mood and style within a space. From exotic blues, deep succulent plums, and romantic shades of red to pale hues of flaxen gold, finding the right shade of granite to fit your design needs will not present a problem. Found within this generous color palette are numerous surface patterns, varying dramatically from the common and predictable speckled appearance, to the fluid movements of the heavily veined Juparano. No matter what your ultimate choice, it is advisable to inspect your slabs in advance and have the fabricator tag them. Surprises are fun, but not when they involve your expensive countertop.

Granite offers considerable latitude in design options due to the wide variety of formats produced. Slabs are cut in thicknesses of 2 centimeters (¾ inch) and 3 centimeters (1¼ inch), as well as custom sizes. Tiles range from 6-inch, 12-inch, 16-inch, 18-inch, to 24-inches square. When choosing tiles over slabs, consider incorporating the larger size. Minimizing grout joints will result in a more slablike appearance.

Texture contributes significantly to the overall perception of the granite's surface. Apart from the easily recognizable and highly popular polished, finishes include honed, flamed, and brushed (see page 155). Each finish makes its own individual statement. The sleek polished finish is frequently perceived as elegant and formal, in contrast to the honed, which is generally viewed as casual or contemporary. The flamed finish is most often seen as industrial, while brushed exudes sensuality. Don't assume that the look of the granite will remain the same when the surface texture is altered. Request a sample in the finish that you are

considering, as the finishing process will often change the outward appearance.

Inherent to granite is a large internal pore structure which causes it to be susceptible to staining, a fact that may come as a surprise to many. Opinions regarding its care vary. Some fabricators seal granite with a penetrating sealer, while others rec-

ommend routine maintenance with mineral oil. Yet another popular view is to let the stone breathe without any sealer, allowing stains to vanish naturally within the deep pore system over time.

Marble Since early civilization, marble has held the distinction and preference as the raw material for the world's greatest

ABOVE: Sunlight warms a countertop of deeply veined mahogany-colored marble.

LEFT: Honed marble takes center stage in this ultramodern kitchen.

works of art and the bones of architectural masterpieces. Its name alone conjures up images of opulence, wealth, and extravagance. With its rich color tones, mirror-like finish, and dramatic veining, marble conveys the ultimate feelings of elegance and formality to any kitchen.

Similar in value to granite in its slab and tile format, marble is a top-of-the-line stone and therefore this quality is reflected in its price. Cost can vary greatly from one source to the next, and while home centers may offer lower tile prices than smaller design shops (due to their ability to purchase in bulk), your available choices may be limited. Variations in quality must be noted as well. If possible, determine whether the stone you plan to purchase is first class (select) or commercial grade. The select offers few, if any imperfections.

The shades of color within the marble family are extraordinary, ranging from creamy neutrals and subtle earth tones to jade greens, tawny browns, and scarlet reds. Combining these colors with distinctive accents, borders, and patterns creates a plethora of innovative and dramatic design options. Marble is available in both 2- and 3-centimeter slabs as well as the full range of tile sizes. Once again, opting for the larger size on a tile project will give you a more seamless appearance.

In spite of its quintessential beauty, this stone choice will surely cause headaches if maintaining its polish is a priority. It is important to become familiar with

marble's negative aspects before deciding if this is the best countertop material for you. Due to its porosity and tendency toward staining, marble requires kid gloves to maintain its original mirrorlike finish. Sealing will ensure that offensive fluids are not absorbed, however, one spill of an acidic liquid will instantly produce a dull etched spot. In most cases, a professional will need to be hired to restore the original finish. If you love the look of marble, but don't want to be concerned with etching, choose the honed finish.

Slate This stone exudes a warmth and texture that is second to none. Slate's versatility can be interpreted as log-cabin

ABOVE: Granite slabs of Gallo Veneziano used on both the countertop and backsplash fuse to form an unmistakable contemporary styling.

LEFT: Neutral colored stone found on both the floor and countertops form a quiet backdrop for the deep terra-cotta colored walls and warm wood cabinetry creating a Mediterranean atmosphere.

rustic or sleek cosmopolitan-contemporary depending on its neighboring design elements. Surface texture stems from the composition of shale and clay as well as the method by which it is quarried. Splitting slate from the mountain by hand allows it to separate naturally into uneven sheets, which results in its characteristic cleft surface.

Surprisingly, this majestic stone can be relatively inexpensive. A typical slate slab will be comparable in price to that of an inexpensive granite slab. The tile format, however, which ranges from the smallest mosaic to enormous 2-foot tiles, will often cost less than many ceramics.

One can almost envision the creative names of colors this stone embodies, such as Indian Autumn, California Gold, China Lotus, Violet Garden, Sea Green, Copper, Rust, and Earth (just to name a few). Exotic, colorful slate is imported from

overseas, as its domestic cousin has a tendency to remain in the less than exciting shades of somber gray, green, and plum. India, Africa, China, and South America produce some of the most dramatic and vivid colors. It is not uncommon for plant fossils to be found on the slate's surface. When discovered, set aside these naturally artistic pieces for use as the focal point of your design.

Options for assorted surface finishes and textures add to the versatility of this stone. They include natural cleft, honed, calibrated, and polished (see page 155). Slate is available in the standard square tile format as well as tumbled, guillotine cut, mosaic, and random flagging.

Employed as a countertop, slate is exceptionally dense and strong. Acidic substances will not harm its surface and once sealed it remains virtually maintenance

RIGHT: The geometric lines on this countertop jut in and out as they trace the angular contours of the cabinetry.

FAR RIGHT: Classical Asian influences are reflected in this blend of black stone countertop and splash.

OPPOSITE: Slight hints of black appearing on the face of the Mexican travertine floor tile reoccur in mass on the angular granite countertop above.

IDEAS for ISLANDS

෨ Give your island a custom shape by introducing a bowed or curved configuration.

෨ Consider a slab edged with decorative high-relief cast stone trims.

෨ For a truly different slab edge profile, take a look at the process referred to as "munching." This process leaves behind a profile that appears as though an iron-toothed beaver had been gnawing on the edges.

෨ Mix and match. Incorporate a slab on the island even when using tile on other surfaces.

෨ Contrast the color and type of stone used on the island to that used on the cabinet tops. A popular combination consists of light travertine countertops and cabinet covers accented by a dark granite slab on the island.

෨ Introduce an inlaid design into the middle of your stone slab. Your fabricator can cut an opening any size or shape into the center, then you can use your imagination on how to fill it. Highly effective designs range from slate, glass, and metal mosaics to intricate decorative tiles and hand-painted murals.

෨ When using stone tile, incorporate high-relief cast stone edge pieces or carved trims. Due to cost constraints, you may not be able to use these trims everywhere in the kitchen, but by using them on the island, you will achieve a high-end look at a fraction of the cost.

THE KITCHEN ISLAND

These serviceable expanses of countertop found floating in the kitchen are more often than not the center of attention. Whether serving as a destination for meal preparation or a casual place at which to dine, this magnet for impromptu gatherings becomes the perfect spot to linger while enjoying a glass of wine and pleasant conversation with the cook. Determining the size and shape of the island is directly related to its proposed use and the overall availability of space. Whether large or small, square, rectangular, or uniquely shaped, it possesses the intrinsic ability to add pizzazz to any kitchen. Because the island is generally intended to be a workhorse, it is a good idea to select a material that can fend for itself against constant abuse. Granite, distressed stone, slate, and soapstone will all provide a low-maintenance surface. No matter if your design calls for the use of a stone slab or tile, the list at right offers some ideas regarding the kitchen island.

ABOVE: A European inspired country kitchen exudes warmth with its mix of earthy hues. The golden brown granite countertop blends harmoniously with the smooth limestone floor and rugged travertine splash.

free. When considering slate as a countertop material it is advisable to choose a tile with minimal cleft or a honed finish. Choosing slate with the traditional natural cleft surface will leave you and your guests dealing with an uneven surface and therefore teetering glasses will be encountered.

Sealing will guarantee its carefree use, but it may be prudent to experiment on a sample prior to sealing the entire countertop. Penetrating sealers typically do not alter the surface appearance, so it may

become necessary to use an additional topcoat sealer, or color enhancer, if you want to bring out the deeper tones from within the stone. Topcoat finishes are available in matte, low sheen, and high gloss. When striving to maintain the stone's natural appearance, be sure to choose the matte finish.

Travertine Evoking a feeling of antiquity within your kitchen can be as easy as adding travertine. Formed deep underground near hot bubbling springs, its classic pits and pores reflect the true essence of old-world style.

The variety of shapes and sizes offered within the travertine family are truly remarkable, and it can be found in both tile and slab formats. Tile sizes range from miniature mosaics to the grand 36-inch tile. It may come as a pleasant surprise to learn that a travertine tile countertop can be installed at or below the cost of a mid-grade laminate—just imagine the difference.

Travertine's color palette normally resides within the confines of earth tones, beginning with the palest hues of ivory and descending down through the rich, deep shades of gold, red, and brown. Its predominant color trait is that it actually never appears as one solid color, but instead the perception is swayed by inherent tonal variations and veining characteristics. Only after laying out a sizable portion of tile do you begin to perceive the overall coloration.

Just as diverse as the available sizes and color tones of travertine is the vast array of surface textures. While honed remains the most popular for slabs, choices for tiles include saw-cut, polished, tumbled, chiseled-edge, pillowed, brushed, bush hammered, and undulated (see page 155). Some of these tile finishes are not particularly suitable for countertop surfaces, such as the pillowed or undulating finish.

The down side of travertine is the tendency toward surface etching and staining. A good impregnating sealer will provide protection from staining, but any acidic liquid spill will leave that dreaded etched area or ring on the stone's surface. In the case of severe etching, a qualified professional will need to be consulted regarding refinishing. Keeping your travertine countertop looking new is as simple as using coasters and cutting boards routinely.

It is important to understand the nature of this stone prior to selecting it as a countertop material. In its natural state, tiny depressions and holes exist on the surface, however there are several options available if this look is not to your fancy. Filled travertine is created when a factory applies stone dust resin to the surface, resulting in a smooth and level plane.

BELOW: The fundamental principles of modern design are captured in the long, sleek lines of this French Blue limestone slab with matching undermount sink.

Travertine can also be ordered in its natural state, or un-filled, and you can request that your tile installer fill the holes with a matching grout or clear epoxy. It is important to note that when the installer fills the pores, slight depressions may remain. As a general rule, the factory fill will be stronger and smoother, but may not provide as good a color blend as stone filled by the installer. The final option is to leave the surface natural and allow it to acquire a beautiful patina over time. Regardless of color, size, or finish, travertine's appeal as a countertop material continues to become increasingly popular among designers and those who seek to capture the essence of a classic aged beauty.

Limestone Velvety soft and smooth with minimal surface variations, limestone conveys a feeling of calm and serenity.

RIGHT: A simple country kitchen features a limestone slab on an iron base as its island.

This stone is often perceived as modern or contemporary in mood, making it perfect for a minimalist setting.

Formed by the sedimentary process underground and in riverbeds, you will often find characteristic seashells and fossils embedded in the surface. While it shares a color range similar to that of travertine, it is, for the most part, devoid of holes and depressions. Cream, ivory,

gold, sand, and smoky blue-gray are the predominant shades found within this stone's color palette.

To guard against staining, it is wise to seal limestone's surface, and be sure to use extra caution when working with acidic substances. Some limestone types are considered soft, therefore extra care must be taken not to nick their surfaces with sharp objects or knives. Some limestones are very dense and hard and can be incorporated with little concern for scratching and staining. Don't be afraid to select this stone as your countertop surface, as it is truly a wonderful material that will age gracefully over the years.

Soapstone A composition of talc and chloride, soapstone projects a soft subtle appearance when used in the kitchen. Its smooth, silky finish is available in both slab and tile format and colors range from ash gray and hunter green to charcoal black.

ABOVE: A deep, ruby-red sink made entirely from marble contrasts the neutral granite countertops in this modern kitchen space.

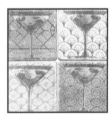

ABOVE: Examples of stone mosaics and tumbled stone. See Chapter 10 for additional designs.

An extremely dense stone, it possesses the remarkable ability to repel stains. You may recognize soapstone from your high school chemistry class as it is used on lab tables because its surface remains undamaged when exposed to most acidic substances. Similar in softness to marble, nicks and scratches can be easily repaired with modest sanding.

Requiring simple care, soapstone should be treated routinely with mineral oil. Over time, its surface will darken naturally. Patience is the key word when choosing soapstone as it generally takes one full year to achieve its full depth of color.

CHOOSING SLAB OR TILE

Determining whether to use a stone slab or tile is usually as easy as taking a good look at your countertop monetary allowance. As previously mentioned, choosing a tile format will normally save you 50 percent over its slab counterpart. After researching available options and obtaining estimates, you may want to closely reexamine your budget to determine exactly where you want to spend the money. Many times, finding a happy medium is the answer. By using tiles on the countertop and a slab as an island, you can cut costs considerably but still enjoy the look and feel of a monolithic slab.

Stone Slabs Capping their cabinets with a breathtaking slab of stone is the dream of many homeowners. If this top-of-the-line countertop is your goal,

there is plenty to learn in order to ensure the investment will please you entirely. Important considerations include evaluating size and thickness, seaming, cutouts, edge profiles, color, and finish.

Size When choosing a stone slab you will be given the option of two sizes: Either a 2-centimeter (¾ inch) or 3-centimeter (1¼ inch) thickness, however, you

can request a custom thickness. Although 3 centimeters will appear more substantial in size, thicker does not always equal stronger. Regardless of its depth, stone is extremely strong, just remember that thicker slabs mean higher prices. Raw stone slabs vary in overall dimension, but on average they are 5 X 8 feet or approximately 40 square feet. Keep this in mind when planning a countertop layout, especially if you are trying to avoid seams.

Seaming It is a reality that your stone countertop will have a few seams here and there, and if your countertop runs more than the average size of a single slab, they are to be expected. Prior to committing fully to your project, it is extremely important to research the company fabricating

LEFT: The neutral-colored granite slab used for this kitchen's island and countertop allows for the more dramatic black and white marble floor to take center stage.

ABOVE: The sweeping curve of this sleek granite bar creates a spacious seating area and a generous surface for entertaining.

ABOVE RIGHT: Polished granite slabs grace the countertops, hop-ups, and backsplash in this stylish kitchen.

and installing the stone. It is not uncommon to request several references, as the overall appearance of the finished countertop will suffer if seaming is done improperly. Conscientious fabricators will cut the slab edges extremely smooth, preferably without a bevel, then butt the slabs together tightly upon installation (less than a $\frac{1}{16}$-inch space between each slab). Then, using an epoxy grout, precisely color-matched to the stone, a virtually seamless look is created.

Joints where the slabs meet can be placed in areas that are less conspicuous if the structural integrity will not be sacrificed. It is a good idea to request a shop drawing, or seaming diagram, indicating exact placement. It is also important to note that highly patterned stones have the ability to camouflage seam lines better than their solid colored counterparts.

Cutouts Abiding by its upscale image, careful consideration must be exercised

EDGE PROFILES

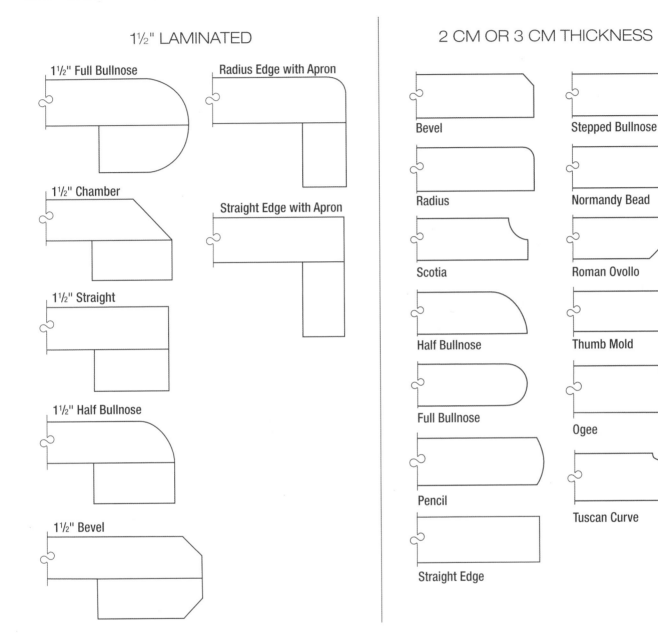

1½" LAMINATED

1½" Full Bullnose

Radius Edge with Apron

1½" Chamber

Straight Edge with Apron

1½" Straight

1½" Half Bullnose

1½" Bevel

2 CM OR 3 CM THICKNESS

Bevel

Stepped Bullnose

Radius

Normandy Bead

Scotia

Roman Ovollo

Half Bullnose

Thumb Mold

Full Bullnose

Ogee

Pencil

Tuscan Curve

Straight Edge

when deciding which cutouts to employ within the slab. Undermount sinks offer a high-end look and ease of maintenance, but carry a slightly higher price tag. This is because the inside rim must be polished by hand, which can add hours in labor costs to your bill. When specifying an undermount sink, don't forget that you can treat its exposed edge to a decorative profile like that of an ogee or bullnose (see above chart). This dresses the sink rim nicely.

ABOVE: A vintage marble farm-house sink adds to this kitchen's European charm. The backsplash is covered with French blue and white tile.

OPPOSITE: Hallia Gold limestone countertops trace the bold out-croppings of a highly prominent sink base.

The kitchen sink and cooktop are obvious considerations when reviewing the numerous options in regard to cutouts. In today's market, additional gadgets range from vegetable steamers, knife holders, and drainage slots to large openings leading to waste baskets and recycling bins. Thinking ahead is a must, explore and research all of the available options early in the planning stage. Many fabricators will want to take sinks and fixtures back to the shop to ensure a perfect fit. Mistakes can occur when relying only upon specification sheets and it is better to delay the job waiting for the arrival of these fixtures than to

be sorry when they do not fit properly. It is also wise to have all large appliances on site when the fabricators template your countertop. This ensures that there will be no unexpected surprises when installation day arrives.

Edge Profiles That wonderful little detail that supplies the finishing touch to the countertop edge is referred to as the sink rail or edge profile. From a sleek, modern flat edge to a multidimensional decorative profile, where does one start? Ideally, you want to observe your profile choice on the same size slab being considered (2 or 3 centimeters), as its appearance may be altered with the size of the material.

Prices start at the cost-effective flat edge then escalate to an expensive laminated edge. Consider combining two separate edge profiles such as a full bullnose over an inverted ogee for a unique appearance.

Color Perhaps one of the most crucial decisions you will make with regard to your countertop will be color. As in all areas of design, color possesses the inherent ability to affect the style of the space. Take a cue from designers and first create a design board. Gather samples of your pre-ferred tiles, include paint chips, appliance and fixture colors, flooring materials, and a cabinet door sample. Include the color tones of any other objects considered permanent fixtures in the space contributing to the overall design scheme. Choosing a counter-top material that blends well with its sur-roundings will ensure a pleasing end result.

ABOVE: The deep gold-colored stone found on both the countertop and adjacent fireplace delicately blend with the pale maize of the cabinetry to give this kitchen its warm ambient glow.

Selecting colors of black and gray will give the kitchen a modern, contemporary flair. Blue and purple will appear exotic, while ivory, brown, and shades of gold lend themselves to a variety of styles ranging from French Country to Old World. Depending upon its hue, green can be interpreted as formal or casual. Deep red and plum will give your kitchen a romantic and cozy feel. Just remember, if resale is in the near future, it is always wise to stick with a classic color when installing something as permanent as stone.

Finish When combined with color, texture renders numerous design alternatives. Options vary widely, but most stones include polished, honed, and aged (see page 155). Each finish projects its own unique personality. A polished surface evokes formality, while honed and aged appear casual and you'll be pleased to learn that nearly all stone types are available in these finishes. For example, if you fall in love with a particular polished marble slab for its color and veining, but a polished surface is not for you, talk to your fabricator about an acid wash. Muratic acid applied correctly to a marble surface will remove its polished finish. By experimenting on samples with varying strengths of solution, you will uncover the exact formula necessary to achieve the desired result. The most popular mix is one part acid to nine parts water. When using muratic acid, be sure to work in a well-ventilated area, use gloves and protective goggles, and follow recommended safety measures. Preferably, request that your fabricator perform this procedure.

STONE TILES

When choosing stone tiles in lieu of slabs, options are virtually limitless. Regardless of the stone, its color, or finish, it can most likely be found in a tile format. Getting creative is easy due to the wide variety available. Because stone tiles are much more affordable than their slab counterparts, you have the ability to upgrade the design by introducing high-relief cast stone edges, carved stone trims, or distinctive mosaics.

Size, Shape, and Pattern Tile sizes range from the tiniest mosaic to the monstrous proportions of 3-foot tiles. The most common and readily available sizes are 4-inch, 6-inch, 8-inch, 10-inch, 12-inch, 16-inch, 18-inch, and 24-inches square. Thickness will vary from $\frac{3}{8}$ inch to 1 inch and as a general rule of thumb, as the size increases, so does the thickness.

BELOW: Dark accents inserted into a neutral-colored splash serve to complement the Zimbabwe Black honed granite found on the countertop.

While traditional shapes (square, rectangle, octagon, and triangle) continue to dominate the market, new alternatives such as the diamond and rhomboid shapes are rapidly gaining in popularity.

On the countertop, tile can be installed in a variety of ways including the simple square fashion (90 degrees), diagonal (45 degrees), offset (staggered), or in one's own unique creation. A herringbone or staggered brick effect can easily be produced when using rectangular tiles. The octagon shape allows for the introduction of a smaller accent piece of similar or contrasting colors. Diamonds and rhomboids can

be used for generating an argyle effect, particularly when colors are alternated, and are perfect for obtaining that whimsical harlequin look. Consider mixing several sizes of one particular stone color, for example, mix the smallest mosaic size of a particular stone with its larger counterparts such as the 3 X 6 inch, 4 X 4 inch, and 12 X 12 inch. Often times using the same stone type and color in varying sizes and finishes will be enough to give you a spectacular tone on tone design where texture and pattern variations become the primary focal point.

Cutouts When using tile, it is possible to incorporate an undermount sink, but this is not always a job for the do-it-yourselfer as it requires a good deal of skill to attractively install.

Edge Profiles The thickness of a stone slab allows for an edge profile to be carved directly into the material itself, however, this does not hold true for tile. Tiles are much thinner and lay directly upon their supportive substrate, therefore it becomes necessary to cover the exposed material.

Several options are available for a stone tile countertop edge, including the use of a complementing strip of the countertop tile itself or a cast stone decorative trim. When creating a countertop with tiles it is extremely important to determine ahead of time the edge profile you wish to use. Because the height of the substrate must be adjusted to accept its specific width, it is

OPPOSITE: Weathered maple cabinetry provides the base for this island slab featuring classic travertine painstakingly detailed with tiny strips of mosaic inlay.

BELOW: Exotic Blue Macuba granite combines with a quiet French limestone floor to create a streamlined minimalist setting.

imperative that the installer has a sample piece on site when the project begins.

If you are using a honed material, such as travertine or limestone, and have incorporated the same material as the sink rail, the edges can be softened and rounded through a sanding technique, resulting in an appearance quite similar to that of a thick slab. This process involves the use of a grinder, belt sander, or special wet saw profile blade and diamond abrasive hand polishing pads. When using a polished tile, such as marble or granite, it may be difficult to obtain that factory polish look. Upon completion of the project, it will be necessary to cover the chalky appearance of the exposed tile edge by using a strong color enhancer. After applying this enhancer (creating a wet look), the stone's edge will shine and blend beautifully with its polished surface.

Finish Tile finishes include honed, polished, chiseled, tumbled, acid washed, pillowed, and brushed (see page 155), just to name a few. Just when you thought there couldn't be another way to distress a tile, something new appears on the market.

Mixing a honed and a polished finish in the same color tone allows for subtle pattern play and creates an interesting dimension. Consider a pattern that introduces a polished mosaic with its aged counterpart of a larger size. The contrast between the formal high polish and the rugged rustic finish gives the design a dramatic edge, especially when interlacing the two in a crisscrossing pattern.

OPPOSITE: Dramatic Rain Forest marble complements this kitchen's sleek, contemporary styling.

LEFT: The drama of a highly polished black granite counter is balanced by the muted leathery texture of the slate tile floor.

chapter two

THE SPLASH

In the absence of a major architectural feature, the backsplash takes center stage as the kitchen's prominent focal point. This confined space between the countertop and wall cabinets is seldom addressed and often overlooked when it comes to creative and dramatic design, but it is undeniably the ideal setting in which to display one's artistic talent. Capable of functioning as an eye-catching element, its main purpose is that of a protective barrier, shielding the wall's surface against the splatter of day-to-day cooking. Because the splash comprises somewhat of a limited area, it becomes feasible to add that extra punch to your kitchen design for a reasonably small investment.

Whether you're building or remodeling, chances are that you have already begun a collection of unique ideas for your kitchen. You may have a folder overflowing with pages torn from popular design magazines or a trunk full of samples gathered from visits to local tile shops. Whatever your ultimate fantasy, choosing your countertop material prior to the splash is always prudent given the fact that it represents a much greater investment and is visually more substantial. Once the selection process for the countertop is complete, be sure to carry a nice size sample with you while shopping. Choosing materials that complement each other and blend well is imperative for a successful outcome. With a little forethought and ingenuity, the one-dimensional and customarily standard backsplash can be transformed into an attractive addition to your overall kitchen design.

SPLASH DESIGN

As you begin your journey in search of the perfect complement to your countertop, you will soon discover that there are literally hundreds of options available when it comes to layout, pattern, color, and decorative tile. This will become the perfect opportunity to incorporate some of those more interesting and exotic pieces you've spotted along the way.

The efficient planner will select the splash material and approve the layout

RIGHT: A tumbled slate and glass trim accentuates a simple splash of slate tile. The countertop is a honed Brazilian slate.

prior to cabinet installation. This process guarantees that the precise amount of space required to accommodate the design is available. Unfortunately, many of us wait until the cabinets have been installed before ever selecting our splash material. This leaves us with the disappointing realization that there may not be enough space

to incorporate our design. If this occurs, don't become discouraged, it simply means that slight adjustments to the layout may be necessary. An experienced designer, retailer, or installer will have the knowledge required to finesse the design into the existing space. In most cases, the final result will be pleasing to all.

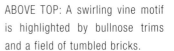

ABOVE TOP: A swirling vine motif is highlighted by bullnose trims and a field of tumbled bricks.

ABOVE CENTER: Handmade tiles in a meadow vine motif create a picture frame border around a field of Crema Marfil tumbled marble.

ABOVE BOTTOM: Mosaic slate coupled with a matching border composes this splash of stone.

ABOVE: A faux finished horizontal wall plate seemingly disappears into a honed splash of Rojo Alicante.

OPPOSITE: A clever combination of rectangles, squares, rhomboids and dimensional trims blend to form a beautiful and useful backsplash.

OPPOSITE FAR RIGHT: This backsplash of limestone tile features unique swirling insets.

OUTLET AND SWITCHPLATE PLACEMENT

With all of the must-have kitchen gadgets currently on the market, it becomes essential to have an ample number of electrical outlets at your disposal. Add to that the multitude of switches required to control all those amenities and ambient lighting and we begin to wonder if it is even possible to create an appealing design that won't be lost in a sea of rectangular plate covers. Building codes generally dictate the placement of outlets. Taking into consideration that they are usually installed quite frequently, creating a seamless splash does sound like a rather insurmountable challenge. With all of the competition for such a limited space, planning ahead is crucial. Early in the building stages or before the remodeling process has ever begun, discuss the placement of your plug outlets and switch plates with your contractor.

There are several successful ways to avoid these intrusive rows of boxes within your lovely splash design. First, you may want to consider specifying that a special outlet strip be installed at the very top portion of the backsplash. Virtually unnoticeable when hidden behind the lower lip of the wall cabinets, it opens the area for diverse options. Second, you may choose to have the outlets mounted directly onto the underside of the wall cabinets, allowing for a truly uninterrupted design. Third, try to locate the electrical outlets at the very base of the splash and in lieu of the traditional vertical placement, place them in a horizontal position. Unfortunately, this configuration will still interrupt the flow of tile, but not nearly to the extent of those installed directly in the center. If you are in the midst of a remodel or update and are forced to contend with the current placement of these necessary features, there is good news. When faced with a multitude of electrical boxes in a backsplash, there is no better medium than stone with which to blend a faux finish. Due to its inherent color and texture variations, a good faux finish can make a wall outlet virtually disappear.

Whatever your aspirations, it is important to consult with your architect, electrical contractor, and/or builder first to ensure that your ideas will meet code and provide both you and your family a safe and secure environment in which to work.

TIPS for the BACKSPLASH

↩ Install the countertop first to ensure a watertight seal and clean seam where the counter and splash meet.

↩ Bullnose all exposed edges on the wall tiles, niches, and ledges.

↩ Install low voltage lighting with dimmer switches to accent your designs and highlight focal points.

↩ Seal all stone surfaces with a penetrating sealer to ensure ease of maintenance.

↩ Allow ample room in your niches and on your ledges to be able to put them to use.

ABOVE: A splash of grapevine mosaic adds a distinct European flavor to this kitchen.

EXPANDING YOUR DESIGN

On average, the space between the countertop and the bottom of the wall cabinet is between 16 and 18 inches. Increasing this area to 20, 22, or even 24 inches will dramatically alter the size of the splash and expand your options. It is important to remember, however, that as the space between the countertop and cabinets increases, so does the height of the uppermost shelving. In some instances, this may result in the top shelf becoming too high to routinely access. The trade off, however, will be well worth it. In the end, the space will not only be visually much larger and grander in scale, but you will have also produced the area necessary to compose an elaborate motif.

Now that you have created the larger canvas on which to work, you can begin dreaming up various unique tile configurations. If you decide to remain monochromatic, employ stones that vary in size, shape, and texture to create patterns of interest. Placing tiles on the diagonal and clipping the corners allows for the addition of dots or accents in contrasting colors and materials that will add dimension to your splash. For more dramatic styling, add specialty tiles of diverse materials such as glass, metal, mosaic, or deeply grooved relics.

BALANCING ACT

You have just discovered the perfect stone slab, its dramatic veining and vibrant color tones blend precisely to make that daring statement you've been after. As a rule of thumb, when the countertop is exceptionally striking and functions as the kitchen's primary focal point, the splash should take a backseat as a complementary element. Avoid using intricate patterns and intense colors within the backsplash when it adjoins a heavily veined countertop. By seeking out a color tone contained within the countertop material itself and transferring it onto the backsplash through the use of a tumbled marble insert or a mosaic border can create a design that will marry the two nicely.

Remember, it is the harmonious blend of materials that is key for creating a breathtaking focal point. Whether you envision a highly ornate splash melting into a countertop of buttercream limestone or a soft ivory travertine accented by a splash of rugged slate, the successful culmination of any design will ultimately rest in the combination of tiles and their relationship to the overall kitchen motif.

NICHES AND LEDGES

When planning your splash, don't limit yourself to the customary flat layout. Think three-dimensionally by introducing something that is attention grabbing as well as functional. Incorporating a niche or ledge into the backsplash area is both use-ful as well as visually interesting. Niches and ledges are generally located just behind the cooking surface or above the sink area. An arched, recessed niche can provide the perfect space for displaying a collection of colorful bottles, ceramic vases, or even a fanciful piece of artwork. When adding a niche, consider bordering it with highly ornate trim and then lining its interior surface with a colorful mosaic or uniquely textured stone. Adding low-voltage down lighting will greatly enhance even the most simplistic of these wonderful architectural features. Ledges placed above the sink can be used for displaying something as simple as a single orchid or as multifarious as a row of potted herbs for the gourmet cook.

ABOVE: A painted stone mural.

BELOW: A colorful collection of bottles appear to float upon a sea of exotic blue granite.

changing the size can alter the visual perception of the frame dramatically. Large, heavy trims should be earmarked for larger frames while thinner, narrow trims should be reserved for smaller versions.

To create a square or rectangular framed border, begin by using a series of straight trim pieces, mitered at the corners. Once you have created the defining border, you will then have a variety of options available for filling the center. Tiles featured in this space can range from tiny, shimmering mosaics to the unparalleled beauty of a hand-painted mural. The rule of three's applies here. When introducing a decorative 4 x 4 inch or 6 x 6 inch tile within the frame, three tiles will offer a much more balanced effect than one or two. For a dramatic arched frame, ask your tile dealer about trim pieces that are made specifically to create this look.

If you are unsure of your layout, it is wise to create a full-size template by cutting a piece of poster board, cardboard, or similar material to a corresponding size and sketch your design to scale. Modifications such as arching the top or moving the sides in and out are better done during this preliminary stage.

SPLASH STYLE

Contemporary Keep things simple to achieve the sleek, clean lines of a contemporary backsplash. Consider using the same material on the splash that is used on the countertop. Keep the design refined by

ABOVE: Tumbled marble simply framed with a dimensional border creates a lovely focal point.

OPPOSITE TOP: Tumbled marble murals.

OPPPOSITE BOTTOM: Tumbled marble climbs the wall behind the kitchen's cooktop. Its varying shades of brown are beautifully accented by the deep relief of the grape vine border.

PICTURE FRAMES

To successfully incorporate a picture-frame configuration within your backsplash, you must first be sure that the space necessary to accomplish this layout is available. If your kitchen theme features a hearth and mantel or if you have incorporated a large alcove in which to rest the stove, you will be blessed with an expanse substantial enough to accommodate most any size frame you envision. Picture-frame layouts may be incorporated into smaller spaces, but should be done on a less significant scale. Because the trim pieces vary substantially in both width and thickness, avoiding disruptive patterns, choppy grout joints, and the use of a busy stone. A perfect example of these clean lines exists in the use of a highly polished granite slab on both the countertop and backsplash.

Old World Jagged cobblestone, aged and tumbled marble, chipped and worn hand-painted tiles; these are just a few of the images representative of old-world style. Whether the countertop is tile or slab, granite, marble, or travertine, the successful capturing of this look is easy. Color choices are best left to the muted earth tones of creamy beige, subtle gold, or coffee brown. Tiles that appear authentically aged and worn will more aptly convey feelings of warmth. It is here that we find mosaics and murals at home in the quiet ambience of a European-style kitchen.

Mediterranean Few materials are as tolerant and accepting as natural stone when it comes to the introduction of the bold, colorful handmade tiles of the Mediterranean. Creamy limestone partners perfectly with cobalt blue hand-painted trims and jewel-tone accents. When

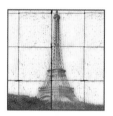

embellishing your stone with these deeply pigmented tiles, you almost feel as if you have been transported to the sun drenched kitchens of France, Italy, and Spain.

Whimsical Shape and color go hand in hand when whimsy is the goal. Alternating contrasting colors in rhomboids or diamonds offers a distinctive effect as does placing tiles in a checkerboard pattern. Handmade ceramic tiles abound in fanciful colors and like most materials, blend wonderfully with stone. Daring individuals may choose to introduce unique collections of items into their design such as metal buttons, charms, or even seashells.

No particular style in mind Try stimulating your creative energies by exploring your favorite design publications or local specialty tile shops and see what styles appeal to you. Next, choose a color palette that pleases your eye. Combine the two, begin to sketch, play, mix and match, and soon you will discover that elusive style that says "This is just what I've been looking for!"

SPLASHES ON A BUDGET

The splash is an area that you really don't want to overlook. When you enter a kitchen with a nondescript backsplash, it almost always appears as if something is missing. Be certain to make room somewhere in your budget for this decorative wall treatment. If you are really pinching your pennies and are an avid do-it-yourselfer, consider creating your own high-

end chiseled look-alike. Travertine tiles can be found in the range of 3- to 4-dollars per square foot and by cutting them into smaller squares and chipping the edges using a chisel or special drill bit, you can create an appearance similar to the expensive 15 dollars per square foot aged tiles. But before you go out and buy enough for the entire project, purchase just a few tiles and experiment. The last thing you want to do is squander money trying to create a look-alike. Slate is another reasonably priced stone and with its highly textured surface and intense color tones, it possesses the ability to add drama to any splash.

Haunting tile shops and local suppliers for overages, slightly marred materials, and samples can be rewarding. Creating a mosaic from discarded tiles, broken pieces, and scraps can challenge the artist in us all. Do your homework before assuming that something is outside the range of your budget, even the most expensive materials are affordable when purchased in small quantities.

ABOVE: Golden Jerusalem limestone is carved with a delicate pattern called Alexandra.

OPPOSITE: Ancient Biblical Stone mosaic is set off by tiny bronze accents in an Aspen Leaf and Pinwheel motif.

chapter three

THE VENT HOOD

Searching for just the right style can be challenging, finding the perfect design element to convey that look can be a major undertaking. When it comes to kitchens, there is one architectural icon that is capable of single-handedly delivering the punch necessary to carry the entire room. That stunning focal point is the stone vent hood. Nothing will set your kitchen apart from the mundane or make a more distinctive statement than a vent hood constructed from stone. Adding remarkable height and scale to the room, their multifaceted character and flair are unparalleled when it comes to defining that specific style. These massive hoods of stone are the perfect complement when it comes to the portrayal of motifs from English manor and French country to Mediterranean villa.

Vital in today's kitchen, ventilation systems work to safely and efficiently remove smoke, steam, and odors associated with the cooking process. Through the use of an exhaust fan, residual byproducts are pulled from the air and directed outdoors through a system of hidden ductwork. Without proper ventilation, ceilings, fixtures, and cabinetry will suffer the ill effects that are the direct result of day-to-day meal preparation. Unless you plan on using an island cooktop with a downdraft system or an above-the-stove microwave (featuring a built-in ventilation system), a vent hood will be a prominent fixture above your stove.

With today's trend of incorporating professional-grade ranges in private residences, the venting systems are becoming larger and more powerful. Considering the amount of space dedicated to this functional mammoth, it is important that it be attractive. The task of transforming this workhorse into a piece of art may not be as difficult as you think. Space allocation will play a part in the styles that may be considered. Small rooms with low ceilings are not suitable for the larger manufactured models, but with a little ingenuity and clever design, custom vent hoods can be constructed to fit almost any setting. If you are in the process of building and a vent hood is not featured on your blueprints, speak with your architect or builder right away. If you are in the midst of redesigning an existing home, sharpen your pencil and go to work. These luxurious architectural wonders are definitely not an afterthought. Your architect or builder will determine ahead of time the placement and size requirement necessary to meet

RIGHT: This simple vent hood, called Provence, is handmade through the age-old process of Scagliola. The splash features a complementing tumbled marble mosaic.

OPPOSITE: Small bricks of Scabas travertine are periodically lifted from their bed to create a dramatic texture.

building code. With these specifications in hand and your ideas regarding color and design, you can begin the shopping process. Choices include structures carved from solid stone, prefabricated cast stone, Scagliola, and custom-built substructures clad with stone tile.

Vent hoods of solid stone are extremely heavy and somewhat expensive, but their hand-carved detail and velvety shadows reflect an authentic natural beauty. Ornate corbels frequently grace either side,

creating the illusion that the massive structure rests upon them. Choosing a substantial hood such as this dictates a location of primary focus. It may become necessary to reinforce the wall, ensuring that it is capable of handling the excessive weight associated with a structure of this magnitude.

Cast stone is similar in appearance, but often weighs much less and is considerably lower in cost. A mixture of finely graded aggregates, silica sand, and bonding agents,

part one | THE STONE KITCHEN

hammered into molds, these look-alikes are often nearly impossible to tell from the real thing. Tracing the simple geometric lines of contemporary design to the complex intricate curves of old-world style, cast stone can be found in numerous shapes, sizes, and color tones. Comparable in stature to its hand-carved cousin, these structures will capture the spotlight as well, so be sure to choose a color and style that blends well with the central theme of the kitchen.

Scagliola, a nearly lost art, utilizes a technique developed by seventeenth-century Italian monks. Based on a secret formula, its cookie-dough consistency is molded entirely by hand to capture the texture of stone with amazing clarity.

Custom-built hoods consist of a sub-structure overlaid with stone tiles. The cost is normally less than a carved or prefabricated hood, and cladding a custom-made form allows for greater latitude in size, shape, color, and texture. When creating

OPPOSITE: This professional-style range is wonderfully framed by tall niches and an enormous vent hood, handmade through the process of Scagliola.

BELOW: Tucked neatly between the carmel colored wall cabinets, this vent hood feature adds a distinct touch of Europe. Interlacing strips of mosaic between a field of tumbled marble forms a "grid-like" splash motif.

these one-of-a-kind vent hoods, consider pulling the same tile up from the countertop or splash to give the area a more cohesive appearance. To spark interest, try altering the pattern of the tiles. For example, if you are using a 4 X 4 inch tumbled marble tile on your backsplash in a diagonal pattern, place the same 4 X 4 inch tile on the hood in a square or staggered fashion for an eye-catching contrast. Decorative trims used on the splash may be pulled up and utilized as a border along the base portion of the hood itself. Smaller medallions or sets of unique handmade tiles can be featured on the hood face to convey the desired design theme.

If the idea of a large stone feature in your kitchen appeals to you, but a towering vent hood seems overpowering, consider the traditional hearth and mantel motif. To create this look, recess the range into its own nook, and frame the opening with a carved or cast stone surround. Flank the two sides with large scrolling corbels and cap the structure with a thick crown-molding shelf. This layout offers the space to display a special piece of artwork, a collection of novel sculptures, or even a pair of small topiaries. One of the added benefits of the hearth and mantel design is a large surface area directly behind the range where you can introduce the picture-frame layout or niche discussed in earlier chapters.

RIGHT: A delicately carved grape-vine motif is featured on the face of this marble vent hood. The back splash is composed of a matching tumbled stone accented by a rust-colored mosaic frame.

OPPOSITE: Golden hues of tumbled Jerusalem Stone wrap the vent hood, backsplash, and niches.

THE STONE BATH

TOP: Mushroom-colored stone envelops this bathroom in the form of tile and mosaic. The sink is carved from dark travertine and rests within a metal ring.

BOTTOM LEFT: The distinctive veins of the marble appear to travel from the floor up over the tub and onto the splash. Grounding the floating effect of the tub is a large square of dark mosaic glass tile.

BOTTOM CENTER: Accents of golden travertine line the baseboards and frame the mirror in this petite bath.

BOTTOM RIGHT: Cross-cut travertine in the color Classic helps to set the tone for this clean and contemporary seaside bath.

chapter four

THE MASTER BATH

At the end of the day, there is a place to which you can escape, to nurture your body as well as your soul; this place is the master bath. Recently evolving into a spalike retreat for the discriminating homeowner, this bath is the epitome of elegance when created with natural stone. Designs are now emerging that were once held only in homeowners' dreams. Arches of thick decorative tile frame the entrance to an oversized steam shower built for two. A deep whirlpool tub sits encased in stone while an enormous hand-carved fireplace casts a warm glow throughout the room. Today's master suite bathroom is no longer the oversized standard bath of the past, it is now an architecturally stunning hideaway that is looked upon with near reverence.

ABOVE: A blend of classic travertine tiles and slabs surround this tub. The soft rounded edges were formed on-site by the tile installer.

THE TUB

Truly one of the ultimate escapes into relaxation is a long soak in a bubble bath. What can add to that experience except to open your eyes and discover yourself surrounded by nature's beauty. Once paired with the shower, the bathtub is no longer part of this space-saving duo of the past. Earning a rightful place of its own, the tub now finds itself in various locations throughout the master bath. Standing alone in the middle of the room, set in a corner, resting on the center of a wall—sunken, elevated, or recessed into its own nook, regardless, the tub is always a tempting site at the end of a long stressful day.

Depending on its final location, there are many options available for dressing up this bathroom feature. When it stands alone in the center of the room, the tub serves as the primary focal point. If it is housed in a wooden frame, you can choose to create a neoclassical look by cladding the frame in stone and adorning each of the four corners with Corinthian columns. If an austere appearance is more your style, simply encase the centrally located tub in monochrome slabs of silky smooth limestone or onyx.

When the bathtub rests against a wall or is situated in a corner, a backsplash is required and offers the perfect space to play with creative tile layouts. When your stone arrives on the job site, take time to cull through the crates to find very unique pieces. Often you will discover a group of tiles cut from the same block that, when

LEFT: A free-standing tub is high-lighted by the surrounding beauty of nature. Roman travertine adds to the feeling that this bath has existed for centuries.

BELOW: Earthy-green slate clads the tub in this tree-top master suite.

placed side by side, showcase a continuous veining structure (most commonly found in cross-cut travertine). Set these aside and ask the installer to run this veining pattern along the expanse of the splash for an incredible effect. In place of large-scale stone tiles, you may want to consider a splash composition of smaller tumbled stones or a field of mosaics. In the center of the field tile, why not add a handsome hand-painted mural bordered in a relief trim or introduce a row of unique etched tiles. Whatever design you choose to

IDEAS for the TUB

❧ When installing a whirlpool tub, attempt to situate it where the access panel can be placed on an exterior wall or in an abutting closet or vanity. This will allow for an uninterrupted tile design on the face of the tub. In the case that the panel must be located on the tub apron, there are several unique products currently on the market that allow for easy access without disturbing your tile design. In addition, a seasoned installer will have a trick or two up his sleeve.

❧ If steps are necessary to access your tub, be sure to choose a slip-resistant stone finish for added traction and safety. Treat these features as a focal point and give them a unique shape or curve. Dress the front edge with a decorative bullnose or ogee trim.

❧ When design and budget allow, place a large roof window over your tub to enjoy the moon and stars at night.

❧ Consider the addition of a floating fireplace at the far end of the tub. Carry the stone used for the splash up and around the firebox. But be careful: Submerging yourself in the warmth of the water and gazing at the flames may put you in a trancelike state.

incorporate, be sure not to skimp on the height of the splash. Many building contractors suggest a standard 4- or 6-inch splash, but the beauty lies in the grand scale, go 18 inches or more to add significant drama.

The *pièce de resistance* when it comes to bathtub design is undoubtedly the large whirlpool tub recessed into its own private nook. Here you can allow for a generous deck with more than enough space to

house candles, scented oils, baskets of soft terry towels, or even a glass of chilled Chablis. Glimmering mosaics can be breathtaking as they climb the walls and flow over the arch of the ceiling. Enhance their sparkle and the overall space with the addition of a gilded chandelier. Do not avoid the addition of these over-the-top ideas, as they will set your bath above the rest.

ABOVE: Tumbled marble, granite, and slate merge seamlessly with the landscape in this indoor/outdoor bathing retreat.

OPPOSITE: Utterly romantic, hidden in its own alcove, this stone-clad tub feels like part of the natural landscape just outside the window.

THE STONE SHOWER

Just as the warm bath serves as closure after a hard day at work, the shower signifies a new beginning. Considered an absolute must in our hurried society, the shower now rivals the tub as the perfect tool for escapism.

Taking the ritualistic daily shower should be invigorating not only to the body, but to the mind and spirit as well. Imagine wandering into a shower clad entirely in the masculinity of rugged slate. Likened to bathing outdoors or in a tropical rainforest, you will surely linger in the gentle spray of water a little longer than normal. When the look of soft femininity is the goal, a creamy limestone tile in a caramel or ivory tone is ideal. Because shower walls offer a large expanse in which to be creative, do not overlook the opportunity to feature a dramatic design. Choose to dress each wall, or the most prominent wall, with a long rectangular frame. Inside the decorative borders of the frame, introduce a field of contrasting mosaic. Within this field of mosaic inset a vertical row of three unique tiles. If budget is a concern, clad the expanse of your walls

ABOVE: Tumbled stone mermaid murals for the bath.

RIGHT: Rugged Indian Raja slate clads the walls of this masculine shower. Adding light to the space is the roof window above and the walls of glass block.

OPPOSITE: Glass, metal, and stone combine to create a unique shower.

- Use a clear or lightly frosted glass as the shower door to show off any designs featured within.
- Consider designing a shower space that requires no door at all.
- Specify a small tile or mosaic on the floor for added traction.
- Place borders above or below eye level for an updated look.
- Consider laminating pieces of stone together for a dramatic crown molding, chair rail, and baseboard effect.
- Add a large stone bench just outside the shower area for drying.
- Choose the same tile size and pattern on the ceiling as on the shower floor.
- When installing a steam shower, slant the pitch of the ceiling so that condensation runs down the side walls.
- Avoid polished marble in the shower area if possible. The acidity of most shampoos, as well as the onslaught of steam, will eventually take their toll on the pristine shine.
- When choosing a polished granite for the shower walls, keep in mind that water spots are magnified on a polished surface.
- When choosing unfilled travertine for the shower walls, be sure to spray a penetrating sealer with a mold and mildew repellent into all of its open pores.

in a large dark travertine tile and splurge on six decorative accents featuring an aged relief design to intersperse around the walls at eye level. Either look is simply stunning.

When designing your shower, there are more than just appearances to keep in mind, you must also consider a few necessary amenities. These include the small seat or bench and the recessed niche or exposed shelf.

The shower seat, as opposed to a bench, is most appropriate for the small walk-in shower. Even the most minuscule of spaces can accept a triangular shaped seat where two walls meet. Creating this diminutive seat takes a little ingenuity on the part of the tilesetter. Normally, they will laminate two pieces of stone together, bullnose the front edge for comfort, and insert the finished piece into the area where the two walls converge. When installed correctly, this seat can hold significant weight. Appearances may be deceptive: Although it may not look it, it is strong.

In an oversized shower, the bench seat is appropriate, and quite wonderful. Dress up this feature by bowing out the center or enveloping its surface in micromosaics. Consider designing a recessed arch within the space for the bench to rest in. Add a roof window or a low-voltage halogen light to illuminate the area. For those installing a steam shower, the addition of an incline to the full-length bench will encourage a long relaxing stay.

When in the shower, you are faced with the inevitable question of where to place all of the required soaps, shower gels, and shampoos, therefore a recessed niche or exposed shelf will commonly provide the answer. Placing a large niche within the center of the most predominant wall is quite an eye-catcher, especially when bordered with a contrasting tile or ornate trim.

The shelf is configured and installed similar to the seat, but on a smaller scale. Your installer may insert a laminated piece of stone where the walls converge and

OPPOSITE LEFT: A sliver of stone tile forms a ledge on which a trio of bathing items are placed.

OPPOSITE RIGHT: Tiny squares of Giallo marble envelop this shower. A stone molding with an ogee detail frames the rectangular niche and traces the shape of the shower walls.

LEFT: Limestone tile in a soft ivory forms the walls of this walk-in shower. The floating shower seat is fabricated from a slab of matching stone.

BOTTOM: The deep, brick-red shades of Rosso Verona found wrapping this shower bench are softly contrasted by the golden tones of Dore Royale marble.

Asian feel. A retrofitted antique dresser crowned with a curvaceous slab of limestone will impart a feeling of romance.

When considering which stone to use for the vanity, remember the qualities each type possesses. The toll of daily contact with toothpaste, soaps, and other acidic substances will cause the surface of polished marble to etch and dull over time. Granite is the ideal choice if a reflective

round the edge for a soft effect. Other options include a precast stone shelf with a dressy edge, a jagged piece of stone slab for a rustic effect, or a thick piece of carved stone molding on which to place an item or two.

THE VANITY

Together with the tub and shower, the vanity makes up yet another essential component of the master bath. Available in a variety of shapes and sizes, the vanity can help define the overall style of the room. Clean, reflective metal stands with cool slabs of pale-colored marble are reminiscent of the classic bath. Ornate amaretto or cherry-colored cabinets topped with dark marble or granite appear elegant. A sleek blond cabinet capped with a thick slice of slate will beget a contemporary or

surface is desired, as chemicals are no threat to its shine. Travertine and limestone are suitable choices, but be aware of possible surface etching. Mosaics and tumbled stone are perfect for the vanity countertop as they will acquire a lovely patina over time.

Sink options for the vanity range from vessels of stone, glass, and metal to porcelain and stainless undermounts to the standard drop in. Be practical—some decorative sinks are best left to the powder bath where they don't meet the daily rituals of grooming.

After selecting a vanity base and countertop, you will need to consider the backsplash area. If a decorative trim or mosaic has been chosen for the shower walls and around the tub, it may be introduced here as well. The splash area can be as small as

BELOW LEFT: Upon the vanity a tasteful blend of gold, ivory, and black tones mix to form the striking granite known as Gallo Beach.

BELOW: Bushhammered stone is carried up the entire wall in a staggered brick fashion. The floating vanity houses a duo of copper sinks.

RIGHT: Recessed into its own arched alcove and surrounded by the soft texture of limestone, this tub radiates romance.

4 inches or may span the entire area from the countertop to the ceiling, depending on the desired effect. If you are adhering to a limited budget, consider running the countertop material as your standard 4-inch tall splash and then border your mirror in something special, such as an accent trim.

The least expensive way to achieve drama with your splash and mirror area is to cut down pieces of field tile (your floor or countertop tile) and border the mirror with it. To liven things up, add a decorative accent in each corner and outline the space between the mirror and field tile with a strip of colorful mosaic.

ON THE FLOOR

The most important factor to consider when using natural stone for the bathroom floor is surface texture. An antiquated finish, a honed marble or granite, a natural-faced slate, these are all great choices for flooring in the bathroom as they offer a secure foothold. On the other hand, a

ABOVE LEFT: A multitude of materials combine to create this exquisite bath. Changing the size and pattern of the golden tumbled marble tiles creates a fascinating tone on tone design. The height of the tile wainscotting remains the same throughout the bath, creating continuity.

ABOVE RIGHT: This symmetrical bath design features a field of creamy tumbled travertine accented by a deep, reddish-brown stone enveloping the tub, vanities, and mirrors.

LEFT: In this combination tub, shower, and steam bath, the outdoors is carried inside through the liberal use of large-scale slate tile.

highly polished stone of any kind is not always wise due to the "slippery when wet" dilemma.

When your heart is set on a sleek polished stone for the bath, consider the addition of an inlaid rug design outside each wet area in the selected stone's honed, tumbled, or mosaic counterpart. This not only keeps you from slipping, but will add a distinctive touch to your space as well. If this solution does not appeal to you, placing a tasteful throw rug outside each wet area will suffice.

CARE AND MAINTENANCE

After you have sealed all stone surfaces with a penetrating sealer that includes a mold and mildew resistant additive, caring for the stone tile bath is no more difficult than caring for the ceramic tile bath.

Choose your stone carefully so that maintenance is an easy task. Setting tiles with a small grout joint and sealing the grout thoroughly helps to achieve this goal.

When cleaning your stone, use a non-abrasive, neutral pH cleanser. Cleaners can be found that are gentle to your investment, and there are numerous solutions that are made specifically for cleaning stone.

Don't shy away from natural stone in the creation of your dream bath. When cared for and maintained properly, the stone in the bath may very well outlive the entire house.

BOTTOM LEFT: Glass tile blends with stone in this colorful bath.

BOTTOM RIGHT: Brazilian multi-color slate adds an exotic mystique to this small bath. A chisled granite bowl sink rests neatly atop an intricate iron console base.

OPPOSITE: A mushroom-colored stone envelops this bathroom in the form of tile and mosaic. The sink is carved from dark travertine and rests within a metal ring.

chapter five

THE POWDER BATH

Comprised of only a sink and commode, the powder bath is a small bathroom capable of making a big statement. Used primarily by visiting friends and family, this modest-sized bath offers the ideal setting for expressing your individuality. Somewhat isolated, it lends itself well to bold and daring statements. Its generally private location eliminates conventional concerns regarding tile selections that may clash with surrounding elements. Combine all this with its guest-oriented mission and it becomes possible to create unsurpassed elegance without worry. Be creative and artistic and envision unique ways to impress your guests.

ABOVE: Fish leap across a splash of glass mosaic bordered by a sandy-colored tumbled stone.

ABOVE RIGHT: A Southwest style powder bath features a floating vanity formed entirely from slabs of pale-gold granite.

RIGHT: This striking powder bath features floors of mosaic glass and walls of earthy slate.

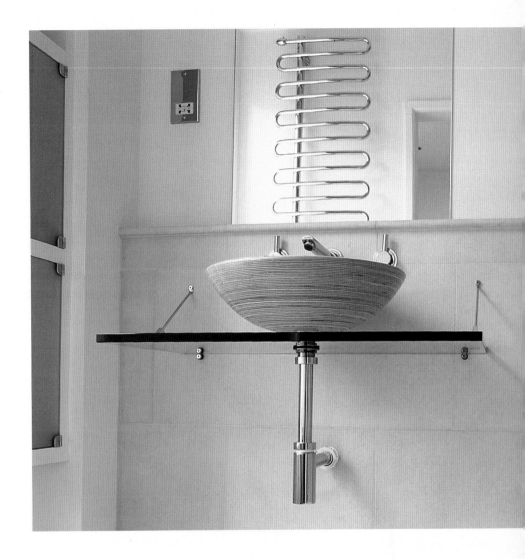

Take a good look at the space you have allotted to function as your powder bath. Ideally it is located in an area that offers a degree of privacy for your visitors and is large enough to move about in comfortably. Because this petite space is generally reserved for guests, it does not suffer from the blatant mistreatment normally associated with the standard bathroom, like wet floors and harsh cleaning agents. Because of this, materials typically avoided may be considered, like those wonderfully delectable polished marbles and mosaics.

What appeals to you as far as design is concerned? Do you prefer the understated simplicity of the contemporary or the classic look of the traditional? Either way, color and lighting will play a major role in the mood and ambience conveyed within this room. Tucked away in some obscure corner, there is little chance that you will be basking in the warmth of natural light, so choose mood-enhancing fixtures to complement and balance the room. Forget the old adage that small rooms should be light in color; select a palette that appeals to your sense of style. A rich, warm shade may be just the backdrop to convey that feeling of sophistication you've been striving for. There are no hard-set rules for this bath, so here are just a few ideas you may want to consider.

MOSAICS

Mosaics add instant glamour to any room. Their color and texture variations are truly mesmerizing. When confronted with a wall clad in these tiny works of art, one cannot help but glide their fingertips across it. When laid upon the floor, your guests will have to resist the urge to kick off their shoes.

By enveloping an entire room in a single-toned mosaic you can re-create the serene simplicity of a windswept beach. The sparkle of highly polished stone mosaics strewn across a backsplash and spilling over a countertop will result in the appearance of a gem-encrusted jewel box. Because of the expense involved in using

ABOVE: Refined French limestone staggers its way across the floor and up the wall as a waist high waniscotting. The large sink basin is suspended on a ledge of clear glass.

Before settling on your final plans, don't forget about the floor. A handful of dark, shiny mosaics scattered across a floor of creamy travertine can be impressive. Consider a border of inexpensive field tile filled with a mosaic herringbone or basket-weave pattern. Normally preset on netted sheets, mosaics are fairly easy to install. Try getting fancy by cutting the sheets into strips to be used as borders or smaller squares to be used as insets. Small custom medallions can also add an elegant touch for a modest investment.

STONE BOWL SINKS

Due to the lack of components present in this cozy little space, the sink and mirror suddenly find themselves center stage, and while we generally think of mirrors as a decorative accessory, dazzling visitors in a relatively new undertaking is the traditionally nondescript sink. Presently struggling to carve out its role as a focal point, this once uninspiring fixture is now thought of in a totally new perspective. Gone is the lackluster sink of the past and in its place is an incredible work of art.

When shopping for a sink, material choices and styles abound at every turn. Your search will unearth bowls carved from blocks of granite, travertine, limestone, and marble; reflecting earth tones of ocher, sienna, and bone. From round and oval to rectangle and square, shapes will vary from the traditional to the exotic and from the primitive to the ornate. Rising to take its place as one of the most beautiful

ABOVE: An elegant powder bath is created through the use of bold colors. The black of the bowed vanity is carried onto the travertine floor through the introduction of dark mosaic inserts.

OPPOSITE: Pebbles, glass, stone, and wood combine to create this gem of a powder bath.

large quantities of mosaic, your budget restrictions may override your desires. Before dismissing your dreams entirely, explore clever ways to incorporate a smaller adaptation of your original design. Remember, a little goes a long way in a room of this size and because volume is scaled down, so are costs.

ABOVE: Slate tiles used as the countertop, sink rail, and splash of this small vanity, add just the right amount of color.

RIGHT: Glass, concrete, and black marble fuse to form this dramatic powder bath. The irregular shape of the 3-inch thick cantilevered vanity top is repeated in the shape of the custom-cut mirror.

OPPOSITE LEFT: Stone encases the entire space of this amazing powder bath from the floor to the ceiling. Changing the pattern from a pillowed brick to a flat square tile part way up the wall adds interest and functions to break up the expanse.

OPPOSITE RIGHT: The free standing sink basin carved from Rosso Verona marble forms the stunning focal point of this colorful powder bath.

design elements within the bathroom is the vessel sink. These functional pieces of sculpture are captivating when set on pedestals or floated above jagged slabs of stone. Reminiscent of your grandmother's washbasin, they are capable of successfully achieving numerous and diverse images. Placed atop a reflective sheet of glass, they appear to hover in space. An isolated sink of hand-carved granite positioned upon a floating vanity of slate will envelop your guests with a Zen-like serenity.

ENVELOPING THE WALLS

Because you may be able to afford a few little extras in this bath, you may want to consider treating all of the surfaces with stone tile. Walls can receive a chest-high wainscotting topped with an intricately carved rope trim or be completely encased from baseboard to crown molding. When

cladding the entire wall surface in stone, visual interest can be added by breaking up the pattern through the use of dimensional trims or strips of contrasting stone. If you

are setting the lower portion of your wall tile on a 90-degree angle, switch to a brick pattern or 45-degree angle above the break point for added diversity.

Due to its small nature, the powder bath gives you the opportunity to stretch your imagination without stretching your budget. This may be your only opportunity to incorporate those high-end specialty tiles you've been salivating over without

breaking the bank. If there was something that you were forced to eliminate from the master bath due to budget constraints, reexamine using it on a smaller scale in the powder room. Remember, through the simple addition of upgraded or wall mounted faucets, decorative inserts, mosaics, or clever pattern arrangements, a rich and lavish feeling can be instilled within the room.

ABOVE: A sink is scooped out of a solid slab of Princess Yellow limestone on this vanity.

OPPOSITE: The amber tones of the mosaic glass floor are repeated in the slate wainscotting of this contemporary powder bath.

THE STONE FLOOR

84 The Stone Floor
From rugged and rustic to polished and elegant

TOP: This artistic floor surface features a hand-stenciled design. By using various pigments upon refined limestone's surface, a cross band pattern is created.

BOTTOM LEFT: A rugged, dark stone set in a random pattern reflects the Gothic styling in this dining room.

BOTTOM CENTER: A formal composition of dark-green marble and pale-hued limestone forms this bathroom's floor.

BOTTOM RIGHT: Wrapping the curve of the landing's risers are chains of earth-toned mosaic borders. The floor is tiled with a classic travertine.

chapter six

THE STONE FLOOR

Natural stone as a flooring material is not a new concept. For centuries stone has been found underfoot in dwellings spanning the globe. From the narrow cobblestone streets of Europe to the slate sidewalks of New Orleans, stone has been laid before us as a pathway on which we journey through life. A great number of these floors still remain in existence today, now more beautiful than ever with the marks of time written upon their face. Their acquisition is so desirable that many homeowners will pay an exorbitant amount of money to acquire an original stone floor salvaged from an antiquated European dwelling. Entire markets exist merely to re-create the enduring beauty of these timeworn tiles.

ABOVE: Vario travertine displays its unique veining characteristics in this open doorway. Darker, contrasting grout, draws your eye to the tile's grid pattern and small natural depressions within the stone's surface.

ABOVE RIGHT: Long rectangular slabs of Princess Yellow limestone form the floor in this contemporary kitchen space.

RIGHT: Antiquated limestone tile allows for a subtle backdrop in which to highlight the colorful furnishings in this living space.

With this in mind, it is a wonder why anyone would shy away from the use of natural stone on the floor. Myths invariably persist and are often times the driving force behind decisions to select a different material. Common misconceptions portray stone as unaffordable, difficult to maintain, or unable to withstand the rigors of daily abuse. In actuality, stone is unrivaled in its strength, presence, and aesthetic, especially when used for the floor. With simple routine care and minimal maintenance, its beauty will grow exponentially over the years. While a manmade material tends to date itself, natural stone will never go out of style.

SUBTLE AND SERENE

Flowing uninterrupted across the room like the sands of a desert, travertine and limestone provide the perfect subtle backdrop for those wishing to highlight more prominent elements within the space. Exhibiting a fairly uniform surface with regard to color, veining, and texture, lime-

stone is the ideal choice for a subdued appearance, fitting for the pared down minimalist setting. Travertine is a suitable flooring material and has the ability to transport you to another time and place. It is important to keep in mind that some types of travertine can look a bit busy with their distinct veining and fine cracks, so be certain to carefully evaluate your choice prior to purchase.

Both limestone and travertine allow for the unmitigated enjoyment provided by

TOP AND ABOVE: Enormous bricks of Antique Grey Barr limestone are set in a staggered fashion. The grout joint is made a bit larger than normal to show off the irregular edge detail.

a natural stone floor without the burden of fencing with distinctive patterns and characteristics present in other stone types. Capable of coexisting amicably with your other possessions, you can cast aside concerns that they will clash with that favorite Persian rug or lavish draperies.

RUSTIC AND EARTHY

Slate is the quintessential choice when striving for a visually exciting floor. Colors and textures are so vivid they almost leap up at you. Rugged cleft surfaces invite you to kick off your shoes and experience the rough texture beneath. Notorious for its ability to withstand abuse, slate is ideal in areas where high traffic and dirt collide.

With its deeply saturated color palette and high-relief surface, slate is more suitably used where it is not in competition with rival elements. If you love the qualities of this stone but wish to redefine its image, try a solid shade with a calibrated or honed finish. This will provide you with an even surface whose muted tones reflect an earthlike foundation on which

you can build any style. At home in areas such as the foyer, hallway, bathroom, and mudroom, this durable giant will add appeal to an otherwise uninspiring space. Becoming familiar with the terminology that describes this stone will help to ensure that you make the right selection.

Calibrated Slate tile that has been machine ground on both sides, offering an exact thickness. Much less labor intensive to install.

Gauged Slate tile that has been machine ground on one side, leaving the top side in its natural state, is referred to as gauged. The thickness of each tile is within an acceptable range, but not always uniform.

OPPOSITE: Antiquated inlaid stone in hues of emerald, cream, gold, and rust swirl together in this unforgettable entryway.

LEFT: A pinwheel design is created by offsetting 12" x 12" slate tiles around a centralized decoration.

BELOW: Colorful slate tile is an ideal material for use in high traffic areas, such as this entryway.

ABOVE: These honed marble floors are so perfectly flat that they appear as one solid sheet of stone.

Guillotine Cut Slate tile with a natural surface on both sides whose edges have been cut by a chopping method. This process creates an extreme texture and ruggedness at the outer edge of the tile.

Un-gauged Slate tile that has been naturally separated without strict regard to uniform thickness is referred to as un-gauged. Both sides of the tile are left in their natural clefted state. Un-gauged slate can vary in thickness from ⅜ inch to nearly 1 inch and requires an experienced stone tilesetter to lay successfully.

Random Flagging Slate quarried in random shapes and sizes. Varies significantly in size and thickness.

POLISHED AND ELEGANT

Reminiscent of a shallow reflecting pool, polished marble and granite lie unwaver-

ing, mirroring the world around them. Adding a rich, elegant touch to any space, these stones nearly always evoke formality. From the classic marble pattern of black-and-white checkerboard to the intense drama of a vibrant Chinese-red granite, these sparkling stones are guaranteed to make an unforgettable statement.

When considering marble as your flooring material, remember that it normally exhibits a heavily veined surface structure and can, at times, overpower a space. Treat it like slate and choose a location where its immense beauty can be enjoyed without restriction or competing elements. Granite exhibits less movement in its surface pattern and therefore can normally be used without fear of antagonizing the surrounding environment.

It is always important to remember that polished stones become extremely slippery when wet and marble will bear the scars of use in high-traffic locations. For improved wearability, consider selecting a honed or brushed finish, as it will add traction and ease the burden of maintenance.

ANTIQUATED

Unequivocally one of the best choices for the floor is an antiquated stone. Because its beauty lies within the fact that it has already been worn, battered, and roughed-up, there really isn't much that you can do to destroy its charm. Its earthy, muted tones are masters of camouflage when it comes to hiding dirt, which greatly

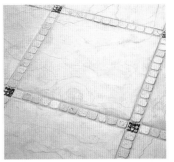

TOP: Criss-crossing the tumbled marble within the grout joints are 1-inch mosaic strips, linked at each corner by a 1-inch bronze Lotus dot.

ABOVE: Dore Royale marble is bordered by a thin reflective mosaic border. Small inserts within the border help to create the popular "rug" design.

LEFT: A marble border and medallion created from the water-jet cutting process grace the foyer in this elegant home. The contrast of the highly polished medallion with the soft matte limestone offers yet another layer of interest.

diminishes the urge to incessantly sweep or vacuum. Its distressed and ragged appearance is ideally cast for depicting an authentic reproduction of many old-world periods. The following terms will help you become acquainted with the types available and their characteristics.

Acid Washed Treating a stone surface with acidic substances to give the tile an aged texture and appearance.

Brushed Coarse-wire rotary brushes are passed over the face of the stone resulting in a texture that reflects a worn, satin-smooth finish, suggestive of aged leather. This finish is tantalizing to the touch.

Bush Hammered The process by which a tile is battered by a machine, leaving behind a rough dimpled surface.

Chisled Edge A chiseled edge is normally found on aged marble, travertine, and limestone. By the use of a chain breaker or special drill bit, the edge of the tile is given a highly distressed appearance, while the surface remains honed and smooth. This finish is readily available on square format tiles as well as random patterns and sizes.

Flamed A rough surface texture achieved through exposure to extreme heat. Often associated with granite and a select few limestones. This treatment

causes the stone's surface to become dull and highly slip resistant.

Mosaic Square and irregularly shaped pieces of small stone tile (*tesserae*), placed together to form unique patterns or pictures.

Pillowed Replicating its namesake, this type of finish creates a rounded tile edge, which gives it a cushioned or pillowed appearance. The effect can be subtle, reflecting a modest radius curve, or dramatic, featuring a deep radius depression. Essential to maintaining the pillowed look is making sure that your tilesetter recesses the grout between each tile.

Reclaimed Original stone flooring that has been carefully removed from the exist-ing homes, streets, and shops of Old World countries. Unrivaled in its ability to add authenticity to a new home.

Tumbled A tumbled finish is achieved by placing limestone, travertine, slate, or marble in a special tumbling drum, along with aggregates, chemicals, or pebbles. These aggregates labor to create a wonder-fully worn, weathered effect by battering the face of the tile as well as rounding and softening its edges. Initially limited to smaller-scale tiles less than 4-inches squared, tumbled stones are now readily available up to 16-inches squared. When installing a tumbled stone floor, you may want to add a color-enhancing sealer or

ABOVE TOP: The soothing blue and gray tones of Indian Thar stone comprise this home's floor. Minimal furnishings and white walls ensure that the stone remains the primary focal point in the space.

ABOVE CENTER: Blue English lime-stone has been used in the con-struction of European homes since the eleventh century. Hints of brown and green in its underlying surface of blue creates its classic coloration.

ABOVE BOTTOM: One-inch squares of Antique Jerusalem Stone line up to form a textural floor covering.

topcoat to draw out the deeper tones and veining buried within its surface. Just be certain to practice on a sample tile first, as each sealer possesses the ability to exhibit a variety of results.

Undulated/Wavy This undulating finish re-creates the look of tile that has survived extreme elemental exposure and endured a thousand years of foot traffic.

TILE PATTERN

Capable of redefining the look and feel of a room, pattern can create the illusion of more space and add character to a lackluster floor. Because the floor area comprises a great visual expanse, it is essential not to treat its importance lightly. Walls are coming down where once they stood, and living areas are being combined, rather than separated. Distinctive patterns and borders are now being used to define each area of the open floor plan, leading and stopping the eye at predetermined locations.

There are numerous tile patterns at your disposal, many ingeniously created thousands of years ago. Take a look around, patterns are everywhere—it's simple geometry. Before deciding on your final design, play with layout. Before either you or your tilesetter get to work, draw your desired design on the existing subfloor, or dryset a large portion of the tile to discover what format flatters the room best.

Basket-weave Setting rectangular tile in such a way to resemble a woven material.

Bordered Strips of field tile or contrasting colored tile can be used to create a border, whether to outline a room or to create a carpet effect.

Brick Style Staggering rectangular tiles results in a bricklike appearance.

Checkerboard Alternating square tiles in differing shades results in a checkerboard pattern.

Crisscross Bordering a square tile on all four sides with a contrasting material of a smaller width results in a crisscross pattern when repeated throughout the room.

Diagonal Tile set at a 45-degree angle to the wall.

Herringbone A pattern consisting of

ABOVE: A blend of white bronze accents and golden tumbled marble tile creates a stunning floor motif.

OPPOSITE: A bright hallway of honed marble leads your eye to a carved water feature hovering at the end.

RIGHT: A Girali Pietre medallion is surrounded by a star burst of Giallo Royale and Aragon Gold marble.

BELOW: The detail of this floor medallion becomes the focal point of the floor.

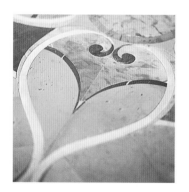

adjoining vertical rows of slanting lines, or any two contiguous lines forming a V or an inverted V.

Modular Many stone tiles come precut in a range of sizes that can be placed together to form a distinctive old-world pattern.

Octagon Clipping all four corners of a square tile results in an octagon where a decorative accent or contrasting dot can be inserted.

Offset Placing square tiles in a staggered pattern.

Square Tile set at a 90-degree angle to the wall.

True Random Setting Setting tiles of various sizes and shapes in an undetermined pattern.

RUG PATTERNS AND INLAID DESIGNS

When a beautiful stone floor just isn't quite enough, it may become necessary to add a major focal point within the face of the tile itself. These flooring focal points

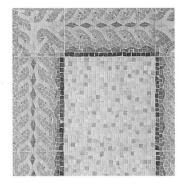

may consist of medallions, intricate mosaics, and etched stones that appear as faded remains of centuries-old stenciling. These elaborate inlaid designs are perfectly suited to areas where the sight-line is expansive and remains uninterrupted. Greeting your guests with style, these designs are frequently found in grand entrances, foyers, and open hallways.

To incorporate a tile rug design, begin by making a template to minimize waste. Making the most efficient use of your material is important with regard to cost. Set the defining frame first. Once the boundaries of the frame are in place, find the center and work outward. Stone selections for a rug project can vary widely depending upon the look you are trying to achieve. For more detail, fill the interior space with a tile that will contrast your

border and field tile. If you are working with a limited budget, create the border out of the field tiles and fill the center by changing its size and pattern. You don't have to break the bank using intricate borders and mosaics to successfully achieve this look. Altering the design through the simple practice of changing the pattern, size, and shape will add considerable interest and excitement.

Astounding for its ability to re-create nearly any design you could dream up, waterjet cutting is at the forefront of stone cutting technology. Waterjet cutting uses a high-pressure stream of water, normally mixed with additives of garnet or other abrasive materials, to precisely cut a pattern via a computer-operated system. This method of stone cutting is capable of rendering nearly any shape or configuration

TOP: A border and field of Adriatic mosaic is arranged to resemble an exquisite throw rug.

ABOVE: A detailed mosaic "carpet" lies upon this lovely floor.

BOTTOM LEFT: Fish leap out of the tub and onto the floor in this beautiful mosaic stone carpet.

BOTTOM RIGHT: A hand-crafted mosaic depicting an octopus is so realistic you almost fear walking on it.

OPPOSITE: Antique Belgian Lava stone form the treads and risers of this narrow stairway.

BELOW : Brilliant blue doors open to frame this foyer's dramatic statue. The black-and-white marble floor design is formed from the waterjet cutting process.

one can imagine, carving intricate waves, curves, circles, and swirls into the face of the stone. Medallions and rug designs cut using this waterjet technique include a variety of materials, from translucent onyx and semiprecious stone to exotic marble and granite.

STAIRCASES

Due to their imposing proportions, the sweeping grandeur of a majestic staircase spiraling skyward is difficult to compete

with, so why try? However, if you are lucky enough to own a home that features an architectural wonder of this magnitude, take advantage of your good fortune and make it memorable by encasing it in stone. Although extremely labor intensive, it will be worth every penny when you step back to admire this work of art.

Treads and risers are readily available in prefabricated stone slabs or you may elect to have them custom fabricated. You need not be limited to thick slabs for the stairway, cladding them with stone tile, smaller tumbled pieces, or even mosaics are all enticing possibilities.

As with any large-scale feature, the ability exists to pull forth a certain style through the incorporation of specific materials. Touches of formality can be generated though the use of a timeless marble, such as the gray and white Carrara. If you seek to capture that unmistakable zesty flair of the Mediterranean, your risers should include tangy sun-washed tiles of bright yellow, cobalt blue, and dusty terra-cotta. If your tastes are consistently more European, thick slabs of earth-toned limestone or travertine climbing the staircase will surely speak of the Old World.

Visually, the size and weight of the staircase will be greatly influenced by your choice of hand railings. Large, heavy handrails and balusters will create a totally different look than an open airy railing of iron. Adding a waist-high wainscotting of

RIGHT: Thick slabs of marble wind their way up this artistic stairway.

BELOW: A simple landing can become a thing of beauty when using stone. Pale-gold limestone tiles used as the treads are softly rounded for a finished look.

stone tile to the adjoining walls of your staircase will add a unique flair, especially when capped along the upper edge with a single strip of polished mosaic and an ornate bullnose trim.

And finally, don't overlook your landings. Stopping to catch your breath will take on a totally different meaning as you experience the beautiful intricacy of an etched design centered in a landing.

CARE AND MAINTENANCE

One of the major enemies of any floor surface is abrasion—stone is no exception. This abrasion most commonly occurs where foot traffic and dirt mix. There are

a few precautions that can be taken to help prevent the premature wearing of your floor. For instance, place attractive and effective floor mats outside the entrance of each door. A well-made mat will go a long way in the fight against dirt and grit accumulation. The average person must take several steps before their shoes are significantly free of dirt particles, so consider a large mat at your main entry, as well as just inside the doorway to catch any remaining particles. Second, get into the habit of dust mopping on a frequent basis, preferably with a nontreated dry mop. You can also simply vacuum your floors, just be certain that the vacuum you are

ABOVE: Stone leaves its random floor setting to travel up the stairway in this petite foyer.

ABOVE LEFT: Cross-cut Vario travertine flows across the floor in this bright open space. The stone tile is set with a tight grout joint and corresponding grout color for a seamless look.

ABOVE RIGHT: Honed Sahara Gold marble is set on the diagonal and bordered by a half tile at the outer perimeter giving the design a clean edge.

OPPOSITE: Large pieces of random stone appear as a jigsaw puzzle in this quiet Southwestern home.

using is clean and in good repair so there are no chances of scratching the stone. Be sure to clean your stone routinely with a neutral pH cleaner, ideally one made specifically for your stone type. These cleaners are readily available at most home centers for a reasonable cost. Steamer vacs are also an excellent way to deep clean your honed (not polished) stone floors, leaving them looking new again. To minimize maintenance in the entryways of your home, consider using a highly patterned design or rug detail of stones that already reflect a soft patina or distressed look. Good choices include tiles

that have been tumbled, brushed, flamed, or aged in any way.

Be sure to seal floors with penetrating sealer in areas prone to staining, particularly the kitchen. Avoid the use of a top-coat sealer/color enhancer in high-traffic areas, as the surface will tend to scuff and scratch resulting in the need to be professionally refinished.

Caring for a stone floor is easy if you select a finish that will not be difficult to maintain. In fact, how many other flooring materials can boast that they can withstand daily foot traffic with very little maintenance and not look worse for the wear.

ARCHITECTURAL STONE

TOP: This exquisite hand-carved stone mantel features cherubs flanking either side of the fire box.

BOTTOM LEFT: A mosaic rug forms the hearth of this handmade stone fireplace.

BOTTOM CENTER: Glass and granite mix to form a sparkling wet bar.

BOTTOM RIGHT: Cast stone columns rise from the travertine floor to hold the circular domelike ceiling in place.

chapter seven

THE STONE FIREPLACE

When the door to your home swings open, there are few features capable of extending a more warm and inviting welcome than the congenial ambience of a fire. Since humans first sought shelter in barren caves, it has been the nucleus around which our lives have been built. Drawn to this element of nature for eons, it is not surprising that we would seek the perfect frame in which to capture this hypnotic spark of light.

THE NEW STONE AGE

Very few decorative features exist that can rival the visual impact of a massive stone fireplace. When put to the test, this charismatic detail generally supercedes even the most exquisite piece of artwork or innovative blend of furniture. Capable of setting the mood and style for almost any room, the newest trend in home design features fireplaces throughout the house. Leaping over its conventional boundaries within the living room to sweep throughout the house like a wild fire, it has spread to the master bedroom and bath, burning a path to the gathering rooms and back to the kitchen, where it originated so many years ago. Once a necessity for both comfort and survival, the fireplace has shed its functional role as a way to heat the home and has transcended into a mood maker, incorporated more for its ability to create an undisputed sense of comfort than to provide the room's occupants with heat.

BELOW: Sun highlights the dramatic textures chiseled into this surround of split-face stone.

ABOVE: The corner detail of this custom mantel shows what can be done with a little creativity.

LEFT: Dark mosaics frame a firebox enclosed by a caramel-colored solid stone surround.

BELOW LEFT: Adding to the natural beauty of this fireplace is an artist's touch upon the mantle.

CREATING STYLE

The fireplace, due to its potentially massive size, is capable of carrying the entire scope of a room independent of other components. Due to the wide range of designs and colors available, it is impossible not to find one perfectly suited for your architectural decor. Lifted from the original designs of old-world master craftsmen, these distinctive hand-carved pieces and their precast cousins represent some of the most impressive surrounds on the market.

IDEAS for the FIREPLACE

⑨ Consider the addition of a tile carpet in front of your hearth. Fill the inner portion of the rug border with a polished marble mosaic or tumbled stone mixed with glass tiles.

⑨ Do not overlook the addition of an over-the-mantel design. In lieu of a painting, many designers are now incorporating these features to complement the fireplace surround. Often created from the same stone, they add yet another layer of interest. Similar in format to the picture-frame design, these eye-catching additions can be stunning when arched, framed by heavy trim pieces, and filled with glittery mosaics.

⑨ Dress up an existing wooden mantel. Introduce a border of mosaic in a vibrant pattern or color around the firebox. These hand-crafted pieces may be pricey, but you will need very few to make a big statement.

⑨ Do not ignore special places within the home for the addition of a fireplace. Since the advent of vent-free gas logs, it has become possible to add a fireplace in nearly any room in the house. The home office, library, kitchen, and dining room all can be greatly enhanced by the amber glow of a warm fire.

Flanked on either side by thick scrolling legs beautifully capped with large, heavy mantels, these fireplaces have the potential to rob adjacent elements of their visual impact. Smaller versions of these Gothic giants are produced in smooth polished marble and creamy carved limestone. With their refined detail and curvaceous lines, they beckon you into a warm, romantic setting. Perfect for small, cozy bedrooms and feminine master baths, these designs evoke a feeling reminiscent of the Victorian era.

Geared toward the simple geometric lines of contemporary design, basic surrounds assembled from stone slabs set to closely hug the opening of the firebox allow for elegance without competition in a minimalist setting. Slightly more impressive but fully capable of conveying the fundamental minimalist principles are walls covered entirely in a sleek polished marble or large square tiles of honed slate. Using a natural faced stone in the same setting will alter the look entirely.

ABOVE: This outdoor living area features a see-through firebox, allowing both the eating and sitting area to enjoy the warmth of the flames.

OPPOSITE: A firebox surround of smooth, light-colored granite contrasts the deep earthy tones of the random patterned slate found climbing the chimney.

 In the master suite, connect the bedroom with the bath by way of a large see-through firebox. Not only will it add a spark of romance to both rooms, but will also give you two fireplaces for the price of one!

 Seal all natural stone around the firebox with a penetrating sealer to prevent stains from soot and ashes and to ensure its beauty for years to come.

ABOVE: Custom made from the Scagliola process, this mantel-piece and over-mantel, Elysee, adds an unmistakable French flair to the room.

ABOVE RIGHT: An enchanting carved stone mantel rests at the foot of the bed creating a romantic ambi-ence in this master suite.

OPPOSITE: An open firebox warms a dining room on one side and a formal sitting room on the other. The delicate mantel is carved from a creamy-beige stone.

Custom-built fireplaces comprised of boulders or rugged stacked stone are reminiscent of the American West and are frequently found in a more casual environment. Consuming a wall in its entirety, these dominating structures make a powerful statement.

For a completely unique fireplace, you can custom build your own firebox frame and clad it in any tile you desire. This is where it gets fun since anything you can dream up is a distinct possibility. Try com-bining texture and sparkle by weaving a 1-inch glass mosaic through a diagonal field of 4-inch pillowed limestone: The effect is quiltlike. Or mix any variety of stones in your own creation. Remember, the fireplace will definitely be a focal point, so make your design spectacular!

chapter eight

ARCHITECTURAL ACCENTS

There is a little bit of a world traveler in us all, yearning to visit faraway places and experience the mystery of distant lands. Actually touching and feeling the landmarks we've only read about in history books, connecting with the spirits of centuries long past. Some of us will make those distant journeys, others may only get as far as the next town, but wherever we go and whatever we do, one of the first places we'll hasten to visit is somewhere that the architecture distinguishes itself from the ordinary. From quaint cottages tucked away in historic villages to the grand castles of Europe, these places all have one thing in common—architectural accents in stone.

CURB APPEAL

Whoever said first impressions are important probably wasn't talking about curb appeal, but perhaps they should have been. Not only must a home's outward appearance be attractive for potential resale, but more important it should be attractive to you.

RIGHT: Stone flooring welcomes you into this home's private courtyard. The slate inlay reflects the ceiling beams overhead. Columns, arches, and niches are formed from cast stone products.

BOTTOM: Warm, walnut-colored stone is randomly set down this stretch of hallway leading the eye to the artwork hovering at the end.

OPPOSITE: Faint gold stone against a strong ocher-yellow stucco forms a masterful façade.

- Placing precast or split-faced stone blocks at the outer edge of your home's façade in the form of quoins can contribute significantly to the European castle look.
- Framing the front door with an ivory-colored limestone portico is stunning set next to an irregular red brick façade. With ivy randomly weaving its way over and around the brick, the look is unmistakably English cottage.
- Framing out windows with stone adds a rich touch to the home's curb appeal. Doing so draws the eye away from the entrance to encompass the entire face of the house.
- Home exteriors featuring the classic combination of both stone and stucco continue to set the bar for homes of distinction.
- Treat your entry porch to a distinct stone rug of mosaics or tumbled stone medallions.

Indistinguishable cookie-cutter homes are rapidly becoming a thing of the past with custom-designed homes working to become the norm rather than the exception. In place of a handful of style options, today's homeowner is given a wide variety of choices from which to create their ideal home. From the entryway to the back porch, architectural accents are being specified in the form of ornate columns, decorative arches, and one-of-a-kind features, helping to instill a truly unique appearance.

THE FOYER

After piquing their interest, you lead your guests from the entryway into the foyer. From this transitional space they should become intrigued with what lies ahead. A duo of columns supporting a simple arch will not only frame the view ahead, but like a valuable piece of artwork it will entice visitors to step closer and take a better look. If columns and arches sound a bit over the top for you, simply framing a portal to the next room with a stone tile and inexpensive cast stone trim can still manage to convey a rich look at a fraction of the cost.

COLUMNS

Columns in and around today's home no longer exist merely as supportive structures, nor do they always fall into the historically popular orders of Doric, Ionic, and Corinthian. Columns are found scat-

IDEAS for COLUMNS

- In areas that need dressing up but do not allow for the introduction of a true column, use a pilaster or semi-circle column instead. Still managing to add character to any space, they are less intrusive and are not as expensive.

- Dining rooms that boast dome ceilings can be made to appear as if the dome rests upon a collection of columns. The addition of a faux-finished ceilings and a crystal chandelier, can create an enchanting dining decor fit for a king.

- Don't overlook the hallway as a place to be creative. This frequently skirted area should hold some interest as it leads you on the pathway to your next destination. The addition of a groin vault ceiling can add a distinctly Gothic look. The intersecting vaults of the ceiling may appear to be held in place by simple rows of columns, adding a bit of drama to this typically nondescript space. If your aim is to be historically correct in the recreation of a groin vault ceiling, clad its surface with small slices of stone or brick.

tered throughout the home for a variety of reasons, the most obvious being style.

Whether used as a decorative element or to camouflage an existing support, these structures make a bold statement and add a definitive element of grandeur to any space. Cladding a round column with miniature mosaics is quite pretty, especially when accompanied by a colorful band of hand-crafted mosaics. Dull and uninteresting rectangular supports can be reinvented

through the use of large stone tiles accented by heavy, prominent borders of carved stone.

The use of columns within the home is relatively unlimited. From private spaces to public areas, they can be found in just about every room of the house, including the master bath and kitchen. For those on a budget, keep in mind that the visual perception of a hollow cast stone column can be just as impressive as a one carved from

OPPOSITE: Tumbled slate mixed with travertine tile forms the foyer's spectacular inlaid design. Light walnut cast stone columns appear to support the stenciled circular ceiling structure overhead.

BELOW: Appearing as tasteful throw rugs, the black and gold inlaid stone carpets lead your eye from the foyer to the sitting area ahead. Framing the view are lavish velvet draperies and Corinthian columns carved from stone.

ABOVE: Stone walls with a worn painted surface create extraordinary texture and interest.

ABOVE RIGHT: The random undulating surface of the ecru-colored sandstone walls creates an interesting backdrop to the woven twigs of a hostess stand.

solid stone. Don't be quick to delete something this impressive from your wish list.

STONE WALLS

For years, interior walls served only to divide and define the spaces within the home. Their lackluster appeal was masked through the addition of artwork and the occasional niche carved into their surface. Now, walls are moving to the forefront, gaining attention on their own through the use of visually engaging compositions. Similar in appearance to the stone walls found in old Italian farmhouses, the new wall of stone features a variety of looks. Contrary to popular belief, walls of stone

are not cold and unyielding, but will provide your home with a genuine warmth and touch of romanticism.

NICHES

Niches, those wonderful little wall indentations heralded for use in the kitchen and shower, are now migrating into entryways, hallways, and just about anywhere that there is a need for an attractive architectural element without the benefit of space.

In the foyer, a stone-clad niche is the perfect spot to house something as ordinary as a telephone or something as daring as a rare sculpture. Niches can be geometrically simple or as complex as a Palladian

🔊 Don't be afraid to use highly decorative columns, such as those featuring a rope twist or one entangled with the relief of a grapevine. These ornate columns used in a small numbers can greatly enhance any space.

🔊 When adding a loggia or large porch to the rear of your home, create an arcade look by placing a successive row of columns and arches along the linear expanse. Bow out the center portion of the porch and treat railings with a thick stone handrail and baluster configuration for that unmistakable Italian garden style.

LEFT: Sets of carved Corinthian columns flank the opening to this lovely sitting room. The Moroccan style arch is created from matching stone.

IDEAS for SMALL DETAILS

- Frame a bland doorway with a decorative trim, such as one that has been intricately carved or etched with an intriguing pattern.
- Dress a doorway with a set of ornately carved corbels capped with a thick mantel shelf.
- Baseboards can be cut from the floor tile itself, or choose to use something more dramatic, such as cut strips of mosaic. When choosing to incorporate the floor tile, be sure to have your installer bullnose or bevel the exposed edge for a nice finished look.
- Consider using a thick slab of stone dressed with a dramatic edge profile for your interior window sills. Check with your local stone fabrication shop for discounted scraps of marble or granite that can be turned into lovely, maintenance-free accents.

TOP: Light, walnut-colored stone trims are used for the baseboard in this home ensuring a lifetime of beauty and low maintenance

RIGHT: Crema Maya limestone is intricately carved with a floral motif to form this beautiful niche.

OPPOSITE: A vestibule is enhanced through a spherical floor design of tumbled slate and travertine and faux finished groin vault ceiling.

arch, mirroring the architectural design of the room. Their interiors can function as works of art themselves when designed using mosaic brocade. Don't overlook the opportunity to add ambient lighting, as it will assist considerably in highlighting both the item placed within and the niche itself.

SMALL DETAILS

Sometimes the smallest detail can make a big impact, especially when used to frame the interior walls of a room. The installation of stone baseboards combined with door moldings and window trims not only serves to enhance the room visually, but also results in ease of maintenance as well. Requiring no annual scrubbing or periodic paint touchups, these features are relatively maintenance-free. Soft, earthy colors and rough textures in combination with the ability to resist wear will result in an appearance guaranteed to remain attractive for years to come.

chapter nine

SPECIAL PLACES

The family home continues to evolve into a unique collection of living spaces, pushing typical and familiar room compilations into the past. New and innovative spaces continue to make routine appearances on the architect's blueprints. The newest status symbols in today's home range from wine cellars and wet bars to meditation rooms and home offices.

ABOVE: A tumbled stone tile and a mural.

THE WINE ROOM

For centuries, families in southern France have spent much of their lives moving languidly between the cool, dark stone-clad caves hidden beneath their chateaus and the rolling hillsides of their vineyards. These subterranean caves hold the intrinsic secret to maintaining the consistent temperature and proper humidity necessary to age their wines to perfection.

Today, almost any avid wine connoisseur can enjoy their own private wine room by creating smaller versions of these European wine cellars within their own home. Costs range from the affordable to outrageous, depending on size and location. First, determine how serious you are with regard to the true essence of the space. If you are not an actual connoisseur interested in reproducing the perfect environment in which to store your priceless collection, you may want to forgo the expense of an environmentally controlled room and simply enjoy the romantic re-creation of an old European-style wine cellar. Either way, the outward appearance of the room will be the same. Rooms clad with stone not only produce an authentic appearance, but also provide the perfect material for allowing the room to be functional when paired with temperature and

humidity control devices. The French chose those subterranean caves for a purpose. Temperatures of 50–60 degrees Fahrenheit and humidity of 60–70 percent are necessary to enable wines to mature slowly. This slow aging process is what helps to generate those wonderful aromas and flavors.

You can duplicate the look of a medieval chateau wine room by choosing materials such as rock, iron, masonry, and wood. Begin your design by making your selection for flooring and work your way up. The floor should visually re-create the aged, worn appearance of a genuine wine cellar. Antiquated stone set in a true random pattern will set the stage.

The walls should carry the look and feel of aged stone as well. Large blocks of split-face limestone will mimic the look of ancient stacked stone walls. Arched niches,

ABOVE: This wine room features a unique limestone called Corton, quarried from under the famed vineyards of Burgundy. Legend has it that its distinct purple veins are formed from a mix of rain water and fallen grapes.

LEFT: A cozy wine tasting room offers an authentic European experience through the introduction of random stone walls, iron, wood, and a hand carved stone bowl sink.

recessed into the wall, complete with vintage bottles tucked inside, capture an authentic experience. Exposed stone walls, ones not blocked by redwood, mahogany, or cedar wine racks, are the perfect expanse for large mosaic or hand-painted murals depicting a pastoral French countryside, Italian farmhouse, or idyllic vineyard.

Some thought should go into the design of the wine serving area. Consider using a small, hammered copper basin in lieu of a stainless steel sink. Adding a full height backsplash will give you the opportunity to work in a few creative wine-related motifs, such as tumbled Botticino marble covered with vintage wine labels or a set of deep relief bronze tiles featuring clusters of grapes. Stemware can be attractively housed in a large-scale recessed

niche complemented by ambient down lighting and glass shelves.

Ceilings need not be overlooked when designing the ultimate wine room. If height permits, add a barrel vault ceiling clad with stone. If this architectural feature is out of reach due to space or finances, consider the addition of wooden beams where tumbled marble can be placed between the expanses and an artist commissioned to stencil a simple faded design.

Should your wine room duplicate the conditions found in those legendary caves of the Italian and French vineyards, it will be necessary to provide a more comfortable area, away from the chill, where your guests may enjoy this sumptuous fruit of the vine. Seated around an antique wine tasting table, lit by a tiny crystal chandelier,

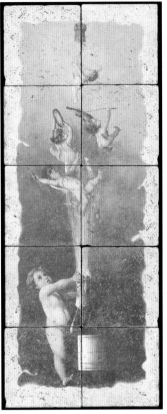

ABOVE: A tumbled stone mural.

LEFT: Split-faced walls and a tumbled stone medallion instill an authentic feeling to this wine room.

OPPOSITE: Antique stone covers the floor in this amazing residential wine cellar.

OPPOSITE FAR LEFT: Small, tumbled stone bricks flow over the arch of this wine cellar's barrel vault ceiling.

ABOVE AND OPPOSITE: Soft, quiet colors envelop these spaces, making them perfect destinations for daily reflection and rejuvenation.

BELOW: A tumbled stone mural.

this intimate setting will allow late night samplings to be enjoyed just outside the cool confines of the storage space.

THE MEDITATION ROOM

Finding peace and tranquility in today's hectic world can be somewhat of a challenge. Uncovering a space within the home where you can escape the windstorm of daily demands can be the perfect solution. When creating your meditation room, look to carve out a small area located in a quiet corner of the home. Avoid extemporaneous distractions like clutter, closets, ornate moldings, and heavy architectural detailing. Ideally your space should be limited to the

simple collaboration of four walls, a floor, and ceiling. If feasible, place a large glass door on the exterior wall of your room that will slide open to reveal a private garden, complemented by a serene wall fountain and koi pond. If your room overlooks a busy road or a distracting view, forgo the idea of a large sliding door. The goal is to create a space in which you can free your mind from annoying diversion and obtain much needed peace and quiet.

To keep the room simple and free of distractions, choose colors that reflect natural light and give the space an ethereal feeling. Creamy beige, soft ivory, muted green, and pale hues of blue will evoke a feeling of contentment. Furnishings should remain simple and unobtrusive. Bench seats of stone accompanied by a narrow table on which to place a single orchid or perhaps a bowl of scented candles will balance the room.

To ensure a serene environment, there is no better choice for flooring than stone. Large-format tiles will limit distracting grout lines, especially when selecting a shade of grout that closely matches the stone's surface color. Use earthy tones and textures. Avoid stones with heavy veining and movement in favor of those that reflect a sea of calm, like that of a monochromatic honed slate. Polished stone may be considered because the room will not be subjected to excessive foot traffic. Highly polished stone flooring will leave you feeling as if you're floating in the center of a small reflecting pool. Sitting on a floor of beige sandstone bordered with a clear green glass mosaic can visually transport you to a pristine stretch of desolate beach. If you prefer to sit on carpet while you meditate, outline the room in stone and carpet the center portion with cork, sisal, or sea grass.

THE WET BAR

The wet bar is not a new feature in the home, but it is currently making new strides in its design appeal. No longer a mundane space to house a few extra glasses and an icemaker, it has blossomed into a visually enticing feature that is certain to capture your guests' attention.

Nowhere does it state that your bartop must be long and straight. When space allows, curve the countertop into a half-moon shape or devise an interesting twist of angular geometry. It will not only allow for a more congenial gathering place, but also adds a bit of intrigue to the lines of

from shiny copper, muted bronze or hammered nickel.

Don't overlook the opportunity to portray creative ideas or themes in your wet bar design. The wall space directly opposing the bar is the ideal expanse on which to work. Through the use of authentic stone accents, you can visually transport your guests to any time or place in the world. Done in style, you will have them all clamoring for their passports.

ABOVE: A French limestone bartop features a Black Galaxy granite undermount sink.

RIGHT: Honed granite is used as the bartop in this elegant wet bar setting.

OPPOSITE: The use of a thin curved slab of stone adds to the contemporary design of this wet bar.

BELOW: A tumbled stone mural.

the wet bar itself. The countertop should be designed to include a hop up, allowing the work area to remain visually hidden from guests. Granite, slate, and dense limestone are perhaps the best stone countertop choices based on their ability to hold their own against acidic liquid spills. This allows both the host and the guest to relax and enjoy the moment without rummaging for coasters and incessantly mopping up spills to avoid etching and water marks. When making final arrangements regarding your bartop fabrication, be sure to specify all cutouts, including a beer tap, if you plan to use one. Sinks for the bar can be a bit smaller and dressier due to the nature of their use. Consider bowl sinks crafted

IDEAS for THE WET BAR

- Enjoy the flavor of old Italy through a captivating blend of tumbled marble, interspersed with decorative hand-painted inserts featuring clusters of grapes or wine bottles. Incorporate a large mosaic or hand-painted mural stretching across the wall. Try framing the wet bar with floor-to-ceiling stone columns joined by an architecturally interesting arch.

- If keeping with the sedate ambience of a smoky gentleman's room, select a dark, masculine stone such as a leathery-looking, brushed black granite that covers the countertops and crawls up the walls.

- Onyx provides an exotic touch to any bartop as its translucent surface can be lit from below. Its mesmerizing glow will surely entice your guests to linger.

- If glamour is your style, gather a collection of pale marble tiles and go Hollywood 1950s! By scavenging architectural salvage stores, you may be lucky enough to snag a pair of retro sconces to use with an expansive gilded mirror to achieve that perfect look.

- For the outdoorsman, use a mix of stacked stone and slate; this stunning combination exudes the masculine mystique and rustic charm of an old hunting lodge. Reformatting the style to represent the Old West will invite your guests to belly up to the bar, western style.

THE HOME OFFICE

Working from home is a somewhat new but rapidly growing concept, hence the need for a specifically designated workspace. The home office should be located in a relatively quiet part of the house and if possible be accessible through an outside entrance. Because this room is a microcosm, it does not need to reflect the basic design of the rest of the home. Your office should be as individual as you are.

Surround yourself with the things you love best. Keep it practical enough to be functional but mellow enough to be pleasant. Using light colors will create the illusion of more space, and when combined with a natural light source, it will provide a spiritually uplifting setting that will keep you alert, invigorated, and productive.

Travertine and limestone, with their subtle earth tones, render an ideal flooring material. Complementary to nearly all other natural products, they allow for a wide range of color choices with regard to cabinetry and desktop materials. Because polished marble tends to scratch, it may be a good idea to avoid its use in office settings, as chair rollers may cause scarring. If you love the wet glossy look, choose granite for your floor or purchase a small ornate rug to place under the chair.

When selecting a material for the desktop, your primary concern will be to use a stone that will facilitate a smooth writing surface. You can immediately rule out unfilled travertine, natural cleft slate, and small-scale tiles. Not having to contend with issues regarding etching and staining frees you up to select marble for the desktop. If a slab is unaffordable, choose large-format tiles and purchase an attractive desk pad.

Be certain that the cabinetry is ergonomically correct in height when you bring together the components of your workspace. Select cabinetry specifically designed for office use. Not all cabinets are equal; height is typically determined by its intended use. To allow for increased depth on the desktop, slide the cabinets forward several inches, secure them, then request your installer to fabricate a wider expanse to accommodate all the state of the art technology. It is also imperative that you supply your fabricator with the precise location for the cutouts through which the plethora of wires and cords will pass. With the wide range of electronic equipment housed on a working desk, it is imperative that their placement be convenient and accessible.

Blending natural materials with a decorating theme, such as "world traveler" or "out of Africa," will ensure a work space that will be pleasing to you as well as your visiting clients.

OPPOSITE: Soft, smooth French limestone comprises the floor and desk top in this home office.

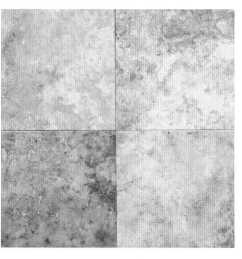

DESIGN ELEMENTS

130

Color, Texture, Pattern, and Shape
Getting creative with stone

TOP: Fan Field mosaic from Ann Sacks.

BOTTOM LEFT: Handmade accents by Architerra

BOTTOM CENTER: Stone medallion from Ancient Venetian Floor Company.

BOTTOM RIGHT: A sample of Travertine tile.

chapter ten

COLOR, TEXTURE, PATTERN, AND SHAPE

One of the many reasons we are drawn to stone is its depth and range of color tones in combination with its unique surface texture. The play of light and dark combined with fine cracks and fissures leave us intrigued by its surface. Those who find they soon grow bored with standard building materials will find themselves excited by their stone years after installation, as it is always possible to discover something new. It wasn't long ago that the options in stone colors and textures were fairly slim. Now we see shades that range the entire spectrum and finishes that re-create the look of thousand-year-old tiles. This trend is unlikely to change as more and more countries are jumping on the stone export bandwagon. Each corner of the Earth offers something special and unique geologically, and this is showcased in their stone.

Exploring the pages ahead will offer you a taste of what the stone market has to offer. These examples of granite, marble, limestone, travertine, and slate are just some of the more popular and readily-available types on the market today. Quarried from around the globe, the majority of these stones are not only sold in tile and slab format, but are also available in numerous sizes, shapes, finishes, and decorative motifs. Stop by your local tile and stone showroom to get the best experience—hands on.

COLORS—GRANITE

Granite began its life as liquid magma within the Earth's core. Created from a mixture of minerals, such as quartz, mica, and feldspar, granite's classification is that of igneous rock. The combination of these and other minerals fused under extreme heat and pressure formed this very dense material millions of years ago. Exposure to additional heat and pressure after its initial formation gave certain granite types their marblelike veining characteristics. Traditional granite exhibits the familiar speckled appearance.

Abyss

African Red

Agate

Amadeus

Amarillo Monterey

Amarillo Santa Barbara

Amazon Blue

Amazon Green

Argentina Mohagony

COLORS—GRANITE

Artic White

Autumn Brown

Azul Platino

Baltic Brown

Baltic Green

Black Andies

Black Galaxy

Black Polar Russian

Black Rose Braz

Blue Bahia

Blue Eyes

Blue Moon

Blue Pearl

Brown Pearl Midnite

Carioca Gold

Carnellian

Chestnut

Cinnamon

Cold Spring Black

Crystal Gold

Deer Island

Diamond Pink

Emerald Pearl

English Teak

COLORS—GRANITE

Forest Blue

Gallo Veneziano

Giallo Antico

Giallo Cabaca

Giallo Florence

Giblie India

Gold Leaf

Gold Nugget

Green Multi Color

Impala Black

India Black Pearl

India Mahogany

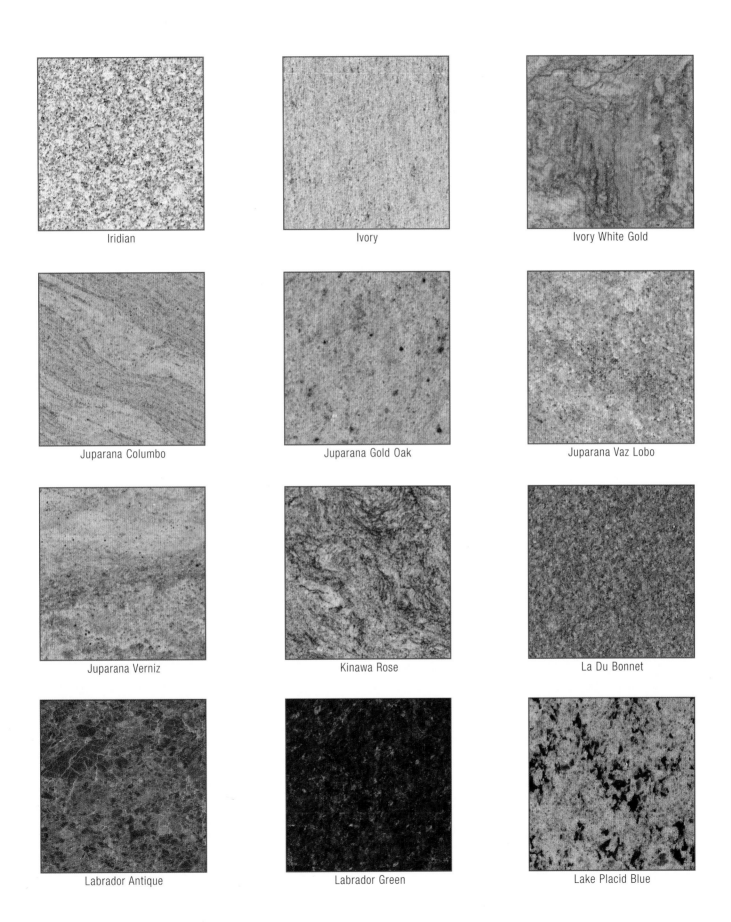

Iridian

Ivory

Ivory White Gold

Juparana Columbo

Juparana Gold Oak

Juparana Vaz Lobo

Juparana Verniz

Kinawa Rose

La Du Bonnet

Labrador Antique

Labrador Green

Lake Placid Blue

COLORS—GRANITE

Lake Superior Green

Marron Glace

Misty Mauve

Mohagony Blue

Mountain Green

New Colonial Dream

New Venitian Gold

Ocean Blue

Olive Green

Opalescence

Ornamentale

Paladio

Paradisio

Peribonka

Pine Green

Polychrome

Prairie Green

Rainbow

Rockville Beige

Rockville White

Ruby Red

San Gabriel

Santa Cecilia

Santa Fe Brown

COLORS—GRANITE

Sapphire Brown

Shadow Green

Shivakashi

Silver Grey

Silver Pearl

Silver Sea Green

Solar White

Sonata

Stanstad

Starlite Black

Tropical Brown

Tropical Green

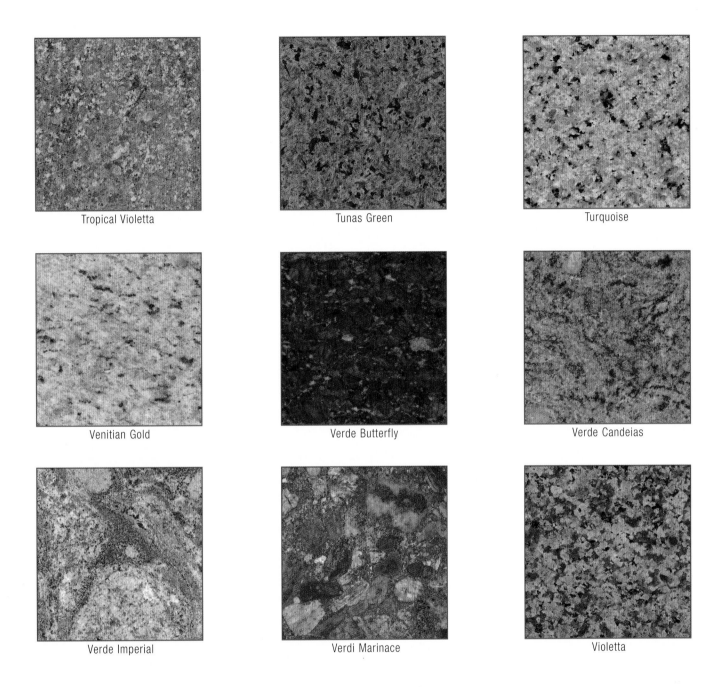

Tropical Violetta

Tunas Green

Turquoise

Venitian Gold

Verde Butterfly

Verde Candeias

Verde Imperial

Verdi Marinace

Violetta

COLORS—MARBLE

Marble is a limestone that has crystallized through extreme heat and pressure. This crystallization process is what allows this metamorphic stone to accept a polish upon its surface. Each marble type exhibits varying degrees of crystallization, therefore the amount of polish each type can accept fluctuates.

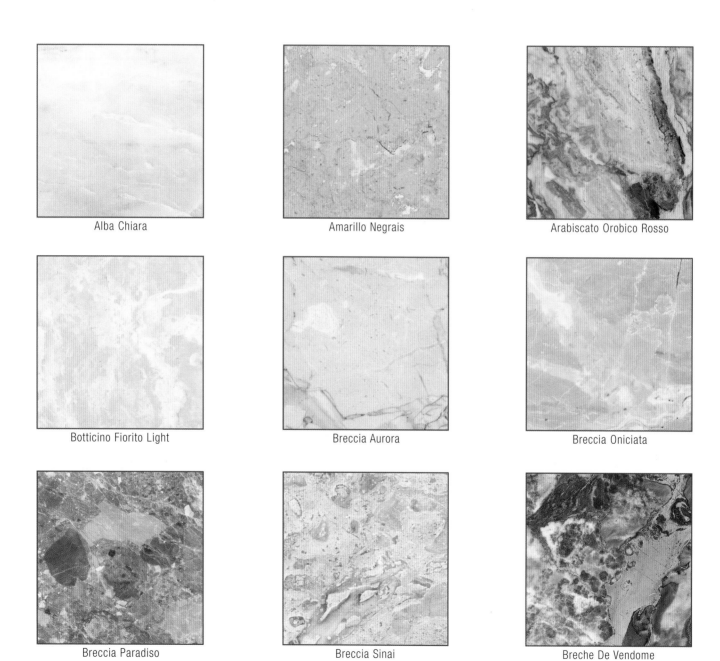

Alba Chiara

Amarillo Negrais

Arabiscato Orobico Rosso

Botticino Fiorito Light

Breccia Aurora

Breccia Oniciata

Breccia Paradiso

Breccia Sinai

Breche De Vendome

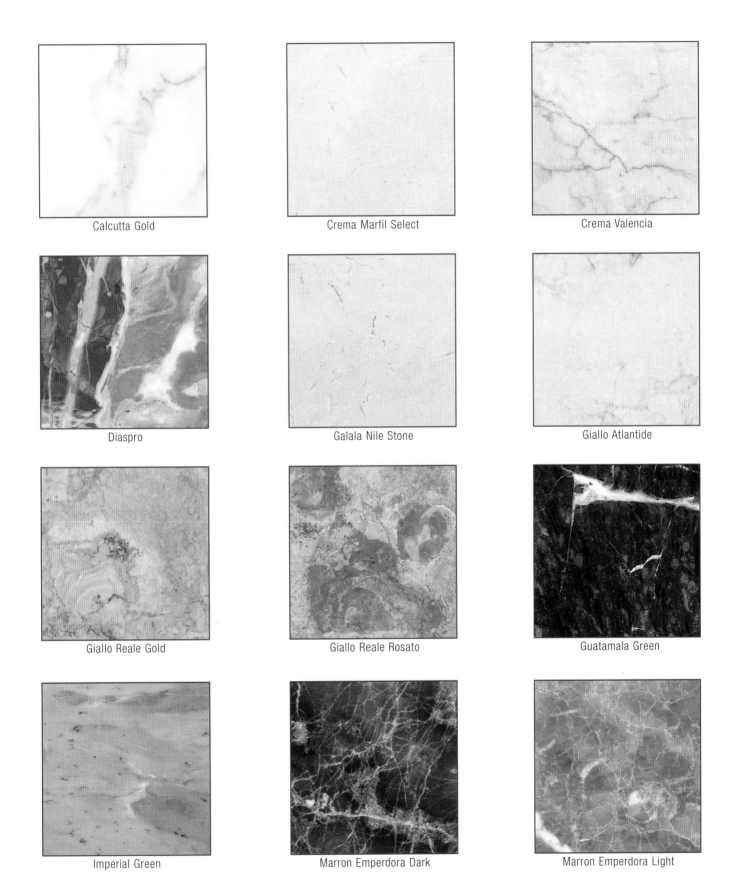

Calcutta Gold

Crema Marfil Select

Crema Valencia

Diaspro

Galala Nile Stone

Giallo Atlantide

Giallo Reale Gold

Giallo Reale Rosato

Guatamala Green

Imperial Green

Marron Emperdora Dark

Marron Emperdora Light

COLORS—MARBLE

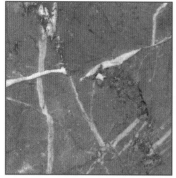

Mystic Red

Negro Marquina

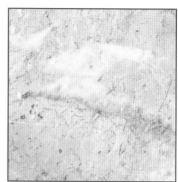

New Giallo Antico

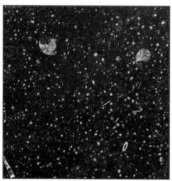

Pietra Di Erfoud

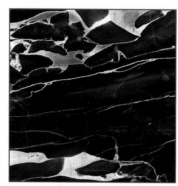

Portoro Royale

Rain Forest Brown

Rain Forest Green

Riviera Beige

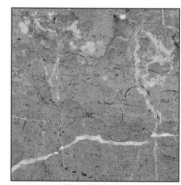

Rojo Alicante

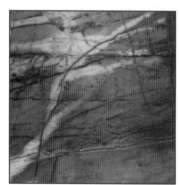

Rosso Damasco

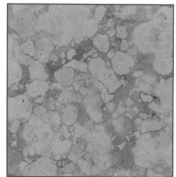

Rosso Verona

Statuary White

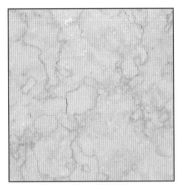

Sunny Dark Nile Stone

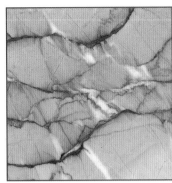

Verde Antigua

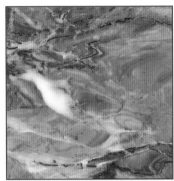

Verde Salvia

White Carrara

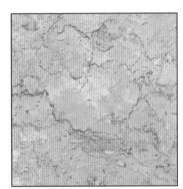

Yellow Dream Brushed

COLORS—TRAVERTINE

Travertine is a form of limestone that features small holes and fissures upon its surface. These open areas were created from a variety of phenomenon, such as gas bubbles rising through its layers as well as trapped plant vegetation that decayed over time, leaving voids in their place.

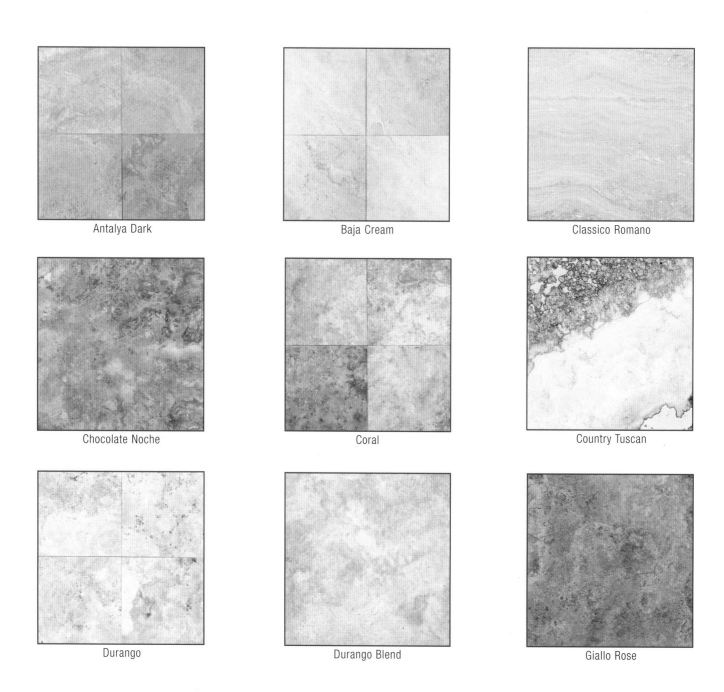

Antalya Dark	Baja Cream	Classico Romano
Chocolate Noche	Coral	Country Tuscan
Durango	Durango Blend	Giallo Rose

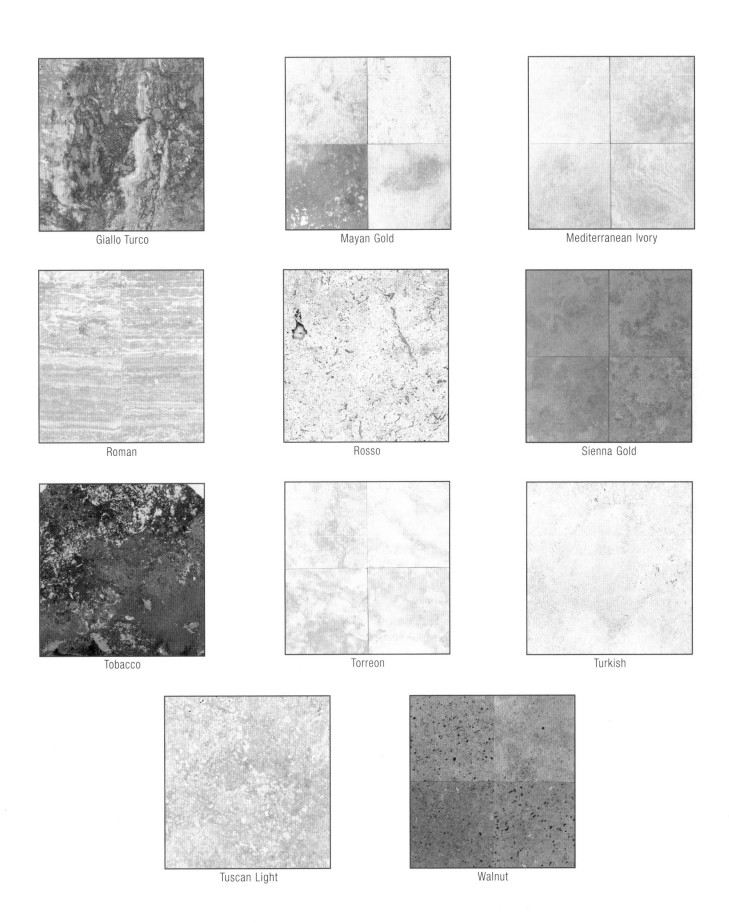

Giallo Turco

Mayan Gold

Mediterranean Ivory

Roman

Rosso

Sienna Gold

Tobacco

Torreon

Turkish

Tuscan Light

Walnut

COLORS—LIMESTONE

Limestone is formed from the sedimentary process, hence its classification as a sedimentary stone. Calcium from shells and sea life filter to the bottom of oceans, lakes, and river beds to combine with carbon dioxide resulting in the basic chemical makeup of limestone, calcium carbonate.

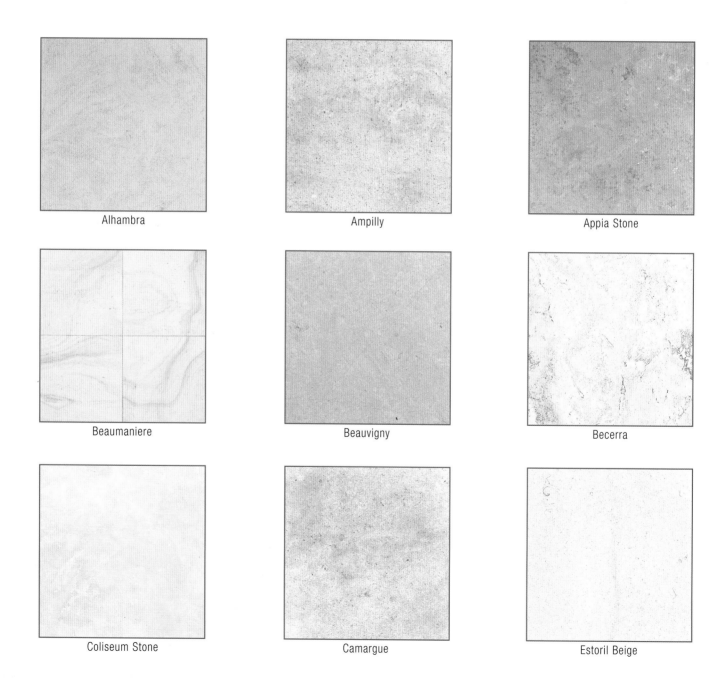

Alhambra	Ampilly	Appia Stone
Beaumaniere	Beauvigny	Becerra
Coliseum Stone	Camargue	Estoril Beige

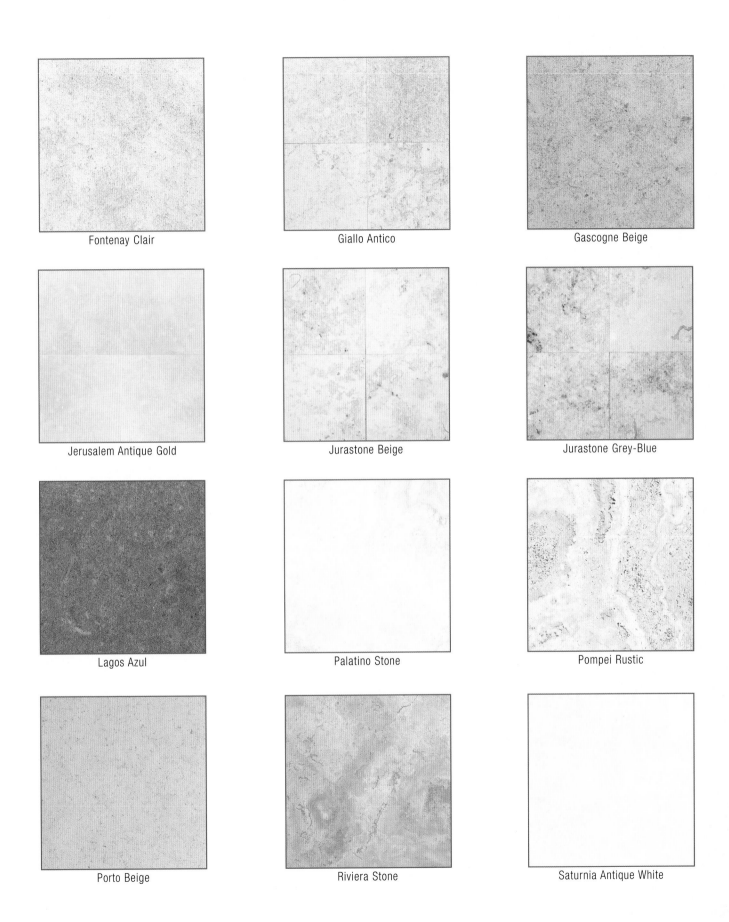

Fontenay Clair

Giallo Antico

Gascogne Beige

Jerusalem Antique Gold

Jurastone Beige

Jurastone Grey-Blue

Lagos Azul

Palatino Stone

Pompei Rustic

Porto Beige

Riviera Stone

Saturnia Antique White

COLORS—SLATE

Slate is a metamorphic stone created from the sedimentary rock, shale. Trace metals found within this fine grained stone help to create its unique coloration, particularly when these metals are exposed to the elements, causing them to oxidize.

Autumn Mist	Black	Brazil Black
Brazil Green	Buff	California Gold
China Apricot	Copper	Golden Sun Random

Gray/Green Slate

Imperial Forest

Indian Multicolor

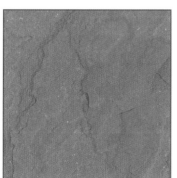

Khud Chocolate Cleft

Mongolian Spring

Mottled Purple

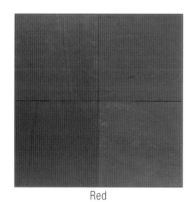

Red

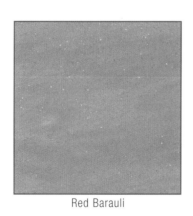

Red Barauli

Red Nat'cleft

Sunset

Variegtated

Basketweave 1

Basketweave 2

Brick

PATTERN AND SHAPE: MOSAICS AND MURALS

Stone is available in endless sizes and shapes. There is no shortage of materials in which to bring your design ideas to fruition. Besides squares, rectangles, triangles, diamonds, and even circles, the most enticing use of stone shapes has historically been mosaics.

Whether placed simply in a geometric pattern or woven into intricate works of art, these small pieces of stone unite to form an overall picture of perfection. Mosaics have been composed for centuries, appearing everywhere from Rome and Greece to Egypt and Turkey. Today we can enjoy the timeless tradition in our own homes in the form of accents, borders, medallions, and detailed mosaic rugs. Often purchased in pre-netted sheets, mosaics can also be obtained through commissioning a mosaic artist to create your own personal design. The following examples are just a fraction of what is available on today's market.

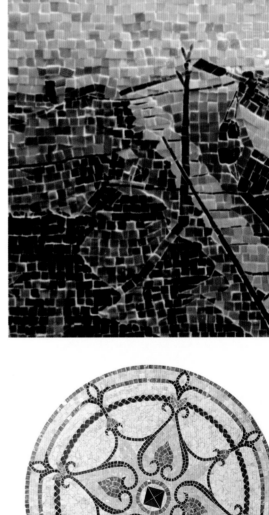

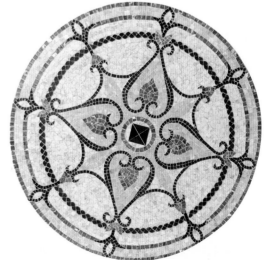

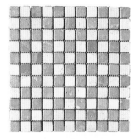

Checkerboard

Herringbone

Octagon

Octagon with insert

Pin wheel

Le Cheval Border

Clovis Border

Pomard Border

Fontaine Liner

Clovis and Cheval Deco Dot

Bourmont Border

Chateaux Border

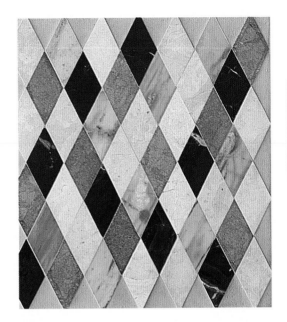

Durango

Orielle

Tiberon Border

Tiberon Decos

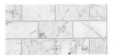

Tribeca Molding

ACCENTS AND DECORATIVE TILES

Natural stone by itself is a work of art and normally requires little embellishment, however, if you want to go beyond this natural beauty and add another layer of interest, choose to introduce accents and borders. Because stone blends wonderfully with nearly any material, these decorative embellishments can range from glass and metal to carved and cast stone materials. There is no end to what you can use to create unique and dramatic effects. The following examples only scratch the surface of what is available. The best advice is to hit the road to the nearest metropolitan area and start exploring tile showrooms. Experiencing the material in person cannot be beat. These showrooms display numerous tile concept boards and normally have full-size vignettes on display. These vignettes give you an idea of how the tile looks in mass and in a true-to-life setting, such as a kitchen, bath, or floor.

FINISHES

Once upon a time, the words natural stone conjured up exclusive images of polished marble and granite. But this is no longer true. The desire for a more relaxed and authentically aged appearance within the home has enticed the market to produce the variety of stone finishes we see today. Thanks to the advent of these unique surface treatments, design possibilities have grown exponentially and finding that right look is as simple as can be. If you long to recreate the romance of a centuries old French châteaux, you can purchase a random patterned stone in a rustic finish or if you prefer the contemporary flair of a soft, smooth limestone in your big city loft, you can purchase large square tiles at your local tile shop. To get an idea of what your options are, take a look at some of the finishes stone suppliers are using today.

Tumbled A tumbled finish is achieved by placing limestone, travertine, slate, or marble in a special "tumbling drum," along with aggregates, chemicals, or pebbles. These aggregates labor to create a wonderfully worn weathered effect by battering the face of the tile as well as rounding and softening its edges.

Chiseled edge A chiseled edge is normally found on aged marble, travertine, and limestone. By the use of a chain breaker or special drill bit, the edge of the tile is given a highly distressed appearance, while the surface remains honed and smooth.

Pillowed This type of finish features a rounded tile edge, which gives it a cushioned or pillowed appearance. The effect can be subtle, reflecting a modest radius curve, or dramatic, featuring a deep radius depression.

Brushed A coarse-wire rotary brush is passed over the face of a stone resulting in a texture that reflects a worn, satin-smooth finish.

Undulated/Wavy An undulating finish re-creates the look of tile that has survived extreme elemental exposure and endured a thousand years of foot traffic.

Bush hammered A process by which a tile is battered by machine, leaving behind a rough dimpled surface.

Reclaimed Original stone flooring that has been carefully removed from the existing homes, streets, and shops of Old World countries.

Acid washed The process of treating a stone surface with acidic substances to give the tile an aged texture and appearance.

Flamed A rough surface texture achieved through exposure to extreme heat. This treatment causes the stone's surface to become dull and highly slip resistant.

Honed A satin smooth finish, exhibiting a flat or matte appearance, as opposed to the reflective glasslike finish of a polished stone.

Polished A shiny, high-gloss finish, normally attained on very hard stones. This finish draws out the deepest color and full character of the stone.

OPPOSITE: This photo demonstrates how the look and texture of Emperador Brown marble is altered with each new finish. From left to right the finishes are polished, honed, tumbled, brushed, and acid washed.

INSTALLATION, CARE, AND MAINTENANCE

Over the years, the stone industry has evolved into a highly technical and global business. Once limited to a handful of countries, where stone was historically the backbone of their building trade, this beautiful and versatile material is now quarried around the world. The growth and development of the stone industry has resulted in more choices and lower costs for the consumer, making it increasingly more difficult to make a final decision regarding exactly which product to use.

Once you have made the decision to use natural stone in your building or remodeling project, there is plenty to learn to ensure that you will be pleased with your selection. Unlike carpet, linoleum, and ceramic tile, stone is a product of nature and varies dramatically from one shipment to the next. In addition, you will find that a single stone is often recognized by several different names or it may be classified as the wrong type, i.e. many true limestones are referred to as marbles and so on. With all of this confusion, you can begin to see why it is vitally important to be an informed consumer when it comes to the purchase of stone.

THE SELECTION AND ORDERING PROCESS

Whether you are choosing stone for your kitchen countertop, your flooring, or your bathroom, it is important to select a type that will perform well in the desired environment. As stated in previous chapters, certain stone types can become maintenance headaches when used in the wrong areas. The chart on the next page will help guide your choices.

Color Variation

One of the most difficult aspects of choosing stone is often what makes it so desirable. . . color variation. As you know by now, stone is a natural product quarried from the Earth. Its appearance is a result of millions of years of geologic change and mineral composition. There are no guarantees when it comes to color and veining characteristics. These factors should not scare you away, you just need to be educated.

Often when shopping for natural stone many consumers base their decision on a palm-sized sample of tile. Unfortunately, this does not offer a true rendering of the overall look of the material. To be sure of your selection, order several full-size samples of the material you will actually be receiving prior to placing your final order. This will cost you some money and take a few days, but it is well worth the effort. The samples on display in the showroom are often several months old and may not accurately represent the current stone lot. In reality, stone changes appearances quite frequently, depending on the type. When selecting a stone slab, visually approve your choice before it goes to fabrication.

Placing Your Order

The size of your order will be based largely on your tile's application and layout. The initial estimate is generally obtained from your blueprints or measurements taken at the job site. Before finalizing the order, the

STONE TYPE	PROS	CONS
GRANITE	Ideal for countertops. Resists scratches, heat, and acidic substances. Can be used for indoor and outdoor flooring, even in climates that experience freezing. Excellent for bathroom vanities.	Granite countertops can stain. Highly porous granites should be sealed. When used as a flooring material its high gloss finish can become slippery when wet. Select a flamed or brushed finish for wet areas.
POLISHED MARBLE	As a countertop material marble's smooth, cool surface is ideal for baking and rolling out dough. Offers an upscale and classic appearance in the kitchen and on the floor. A beautiful soft matte patina will emerge when left to age naturally. Fitting for the elegant powder bath.	When used as a countertop surface marble will scratch, stain and etch easily. On interior floors, dirt and sand will dull its shine over time. Not recommended for outdoor flooring and slippery when wet. In the shower, acidic soaps and shampoos will etch its polish and water spots will be magnified.
SLATE	As a countertop material, slate does not react with acids and resists staining. Will take significant abuse as a flooring material and inherent color variations camouflage dirt. Ideal for the bathroom and shower. Offers sure footing when wet.	Natural cleft slate can become a nuisance when used as the countertop due to its uneven surface. Sealing helps ensure its carefree use.
LIMESTONE	Limestone is a durable countertop material when selecting from the harder and denser types. These harder stones function similar to granite. Perfect for floors in the bathroom and shower. Offers sure footing when wet.	Soft, porous limestone can scratch, stain, and etch more easily than the denser varieties. Sealing these softer stones will help to prevent staining but will not stop problems with etching and scratching. Penetrating sealer should be applied to countertops, floors, and wet areas. Not recommended for outdoor flooring in climates prone to freezing.
TRAVERTINE	Travertine is an appropriate countertop material when selecting from the harder, denser varieties. It can be ordered factory filled for a uniform countertop surface. Ideal for floors and in the bathroom. Can be used in the shower. Offers sure footing when wet.	Softer, porous varieties can scratch, stain, and etch more easily than the denser varieties. Must seal for stain prevention on countertops. Requires a penetrating sealer in high traffic and wet areas. Not recommended as outdoor flooring in climates that experience freezing.

estimated quantities should be confirmed by the installer who will be doing the work. The old adage that two heads are better than one definitely applies to the ordering process and can effectively reduce the chance of error on the part of either the dealer or the installer. When in doubt, go with the tile installer's estimate. If their numbers seem slightly higher, it is because they normally add five to ten percent more material to cover breakage and waste. This percentage varies depending on the complexity of the installation itself. Jobs that include a large number of angles and require numerous cuts will result in more waste. A good illustration compares stone laid diagonally versus stone laid square. Because the corners must be cut in the diagonal application it will require more stone to cover an identical surface area.

It is always important to order more material than you need. Running short of tile in the middle of a project can cause significant problems and delays. There is the potential that when you place the order for the remaining quantity needed, the supplier may be out of stock or the new material may not be a perfect color match. Should you need to make any future repairs, you will need extra material on hand, as it would be nearly impossible to find the same stone in the same color several years down the line.

Receiving Your Stone

When you receive your material inspect it thoroughly to see that it has not been damaged during shipment and that it is the stone you ordered. Because stone tile is extremely heavy and can shift during shipment, some minimal breakage should be expected. Generally, this does not impact the overall coverage as broken pieces can be used in areas that require the stone to be cut. However, should the breakage be extensive, it must be reported to the dealer and freight carrier immediately. Due to the extreme weight of stone, freight carriers typically discount charges up to 70 percent. These deep discounts do not come without a trade off. Normally, a freight carrier only insures the merchandise up to the discounted price, or in this example, 30 percent of the value. For this reason it is important that you know the dealer's and their supplier's policy regarding severely damaged materials. To ease your mind, it is extremely rare to receive a shipment that has substantial damages. Most people will never encounter such a problem.

When your stone arrives, be aware that the crates are often stored outside, and may be damp. This will result in the tiles appearing much darker than the samples from which you selected. Before you contact your dealer regarding a shipping error, pull several pieces from the crate and allow

them to dry for several hours. You will discover that they will lighten significantly.
On the opposite end of the spectrum, stone
often arrives dusty and dry and requires
cleaning to resemble the showroom sample.

If for some reason you are not satisfied
with the material once it has been received
or you have changed your mind all together
regarding your selection, you will more
than likely face a restocking fee to cover
the cost of returning the shipment to the
supplier. Returning crates of stone is a
cumbersome and costly job, so make sure
that you have done your homework prior
to placing your order.

HIRING A GOOD INSTALLER

Very few things have the ability to impact
the final appearance of a stone application
more than the skills of the installer. Therefore, hiring a qualified tradesman is imperative. Unless you are familiar with the
work of a particular tilesetter, it is wise to
interview several before signing a contract.
During the interview process ask about the
number of years experience working with
natural stone. It is important to note that
the installation of natural stone tile varies
tremendously from that of ceramic tile.
Even the most talented and experienced
ceramic tilesetter can struggle with a stone
application. Request references and if possible view a sample of his or her work. Also,

it is a good idea to have a rough estimate of
the going rate for stone installations in your
area. Setting stone tile normally costs more
than ceramic. This is due, in part, to the
extra labor and materials involved. A quote
that seems either much too high or too low
should be approached with caution. If you
have received an installed quote from your
stone dealer, insist on interviewing the
tilesetter who will be doing the work before
proceeding. A good stone setter is an artist
who will magnify the beauty of an already
exquisite work of nature. If you are a
do-it-yourselfer, we will be discussing your
challenges in the next section. Even if you
have absolutely no desire to lay your own
stone, read this section anyway; a little bit of
knowledge will go a long way toward helping you evaluate your prospective installer
candidates during the interview process.

After you have selected your tile setter,
be sure that you know exactly what is
included in the cost of installation, and
request it in writing. Most tradespeople
will include in their bid all of the material
needed to complete the project, including
preparing the surface, setting the material,
grouting, and sealing. Surface preparation
should include cleaning the area and level-
ing if necessary, installing cement board or
floating material for floors that are not on
concrete foundations, installing plywood
and cement board on countertops, and
installing crack suppressant membrane

where needed. Setting materials include the mortar and any additives that may be required. Also included in the bid should be the grout and sealants that are needed to finish and protect the application.

Finally, ask your tile setter if he or she is insured. If licensing is required in your area, request to see the license as well. If a crew is employed, make certain that the crew is covered by worker's compensation in your state. The last thing you need is to be forced to shut down your job due to worker's comp violations.

It is customary for tradespeople to ask for monetary draws as the job progresses. Never pay for an entire job up front. Try to work out a three-part payment system. The first third should be paid up front, the second when the work reaches the halfway point, and the final third draw upon satisfactory completion of the project. Do not enter into any agreement without a written contract that details the installation, identifies the warranty period, and spells out exactly what is covered under the warranty.

DOING IT YOURSELF

Ideally, if you are a do-it-yourselfer, you already have a pretty good handle on setting ceramic tile. If not, it may be wise to pick up a book or video on laying tile in general, as this section addresses the special intricacies of setting stone and assumes that you are familiar with basics. Before we even begin this section, we need to caution you that properly laying natural stone is a tough job. Even improperly laying natural stone is hard work. It will not only test your knees, back, hands, and muscles in a trial of endurance, but in pain as well. If you experience chronic knee or back problems and your application is on the floor, you may want to reconsider taking on the job of installation. An average 18-inch stone tile can weigh upward of fifteen pounds. If your confidence level is still running high and you remain steadfast in your decision, be forewarned that laying stone is an intricate, time-consuming, and detailed job. Still not discouraged? Then let's begin with the equipment that you will need.

TOOLS OF THE TRADE

Angle Grinder A hand held, high-speed tool that resembles a buffer, but has a diamond wheel instead. Its primary use is to make intricate cuts that would be extremely difficult on a traditional wet saw. This grinder is typically fitted with a 4-inch diamond blade and can also be used to shape exposed tile edges as well.

Back Brace Even if your back is in good shape when beginning your stone installation, it may not be when you're finished. Be careful and take a few simple precautions like wearing a back brace and lifting correctly.

Grout Float Used to force grout into tile joints or surface holes. The rubber edge makes a flush contact with the tile surface removing excess grout while forcing the majority of it into the recesses of the surface.

Grout Joint Spacers Available in various sizes, these rubber or plastic pieces are used to maintain a precise grout joint between each tile. When laying stone use a $\frac{1}{16}$-inch spacer. Grout joint spacers are not necessary in applications where the tiles are being laid directly next to each other in what is commonly referred to as "butt jointed."

Grout Sponges These durable sponges are designed for cleaning grout and/or mortar from a tile's surface. They are essential for removing any excess mortar that may have been left behind during installation, or residual grout that if left to dry results in an unattractive, filmy haze.

Jamb Saw A tool specifically designed for trimming the bottom portion of door-jambs, allowing tiles to fit beneath them easily. The handle of this saw is positioned on the top allowing for the blade to glide over the surface of a tile. Its design permits you to place the tile adjacent to the jamb and make a precision cut that will match its depth. Remember, mortar adds slightly to the finished height of an installed tile.

Knee Pads An essential accessory for protecting your knees during floor applications. Do not skimp here, purchasing quality knee pads to begin with will save you a trip when your bruised, achy knees send you scurrying back to the store to purchase new ones.

Margin Trowel A small, un-notched trowel that is used for applying mortar in hard-to-reach areas. This trowel can also be used to back-butter tiles. (Back-buttering will be discussed a little later on in the installation section).

Mortar Mixing Paddle Although the setting material can be mixed by hand, a mixing paddle can make the process much faster and easier. Mixing paddles work best with a heavy-duty $\frac{1}{2}$-inch electric drill.

Mortar Trowel This is the trowel you will use to apply the setting material to the surface receiving the stone. These trowels are available with notches or grooves that vary in depth and width. Typically, the smaller and lighter the stone, the shallower the notch should be. Large, heavy stone will require a trowel with deeper and wider notches. A good rule of thumb is to use a notch size that corresponds with the thickness of the tile, i.e., use a $\frac{1}{4}$-inch notched trowel for a $\frac{1}{4}$-inch thick stone and a $\frac{1}{2}$-inch notched trowel for a $\frac{1}{2}$-inch thick stone. Normally, the larger the stone tile, the thicker it becomes.

Water Buckets Used to clean up both excess mortar and grout. It is important to have several buckets filled with clean, clear water conveniently located in the work area.

Wet Saw A wet saw with a diamond blade is essential for cutting stone. These saws can be purchased if you think more tile projects are in your future or if the job will be continued over a long period of time. But, if the job can be completed in a weekend, consider renting. Wet saws are available at most equipment rental companies and home improvement centers. For smaller projects, a tabletop saw can be purchased for under 150 dollars. While these saws are perfect for small jobs, they may not be a good choice when it comes to cutting large-format tiles or for sizeable projects. A saw with a 10-inch diamond blade and water tub reservoir that features a water pump is best for larger applications. These larger saws can also be purchased, but are considerably more expensive. They are available at home improvement centers, tile specialty stores, by mail order, and via the Internet.

Other Needed Items Common tools such as a 4-foot level, chalk line, square, pencil, and measuring tape will also be required.

Once you have gathered, borrowed, or purchased the equipment you will need to do the job, you really can't look back. Take a deep breath, take your time, and do a professional job. Next we will discuss the preparation needed before beginning the job of installation.

Surface Preparation

Countertops Specific countertop preparation is required to provide the structural integrity necessary to support the weight of stone, ensure a level surface, and create the desired depth for your edge profile.

Materials used in this preparation include plywood, wood adhesive, cement board, and screws. Good quality ¾-inch plywood should cover the cabinet tops, with additional layers of plywood laminated to it with screws and adhesive. A final layer of cement board is then installed to serve as the tile bonding surface.

Remember that the combined depth of the plywood, cement board, mortar, and tile will dictate the thickness of the countertop edge. If you plan on using a manufactured edge, make sure that the combined thickness of materials, including the tile, is slightly less than the edge being used.

Don't forget to make sure that your countertop is level. If the cabinets were installed out of level to begin with, shims will be necessary to level the countertop.

Countertop Backsplash If this is new construction, cement board should be screwed directly onto the wall studs. If this is a remodel, the splash tiles can be set on the existing surface. If it is possible to pull the receptacle boxes forward, a thin sheet of cement board can effectively be installed directly over the top of existing drywall and screwed into the studs as well. If you chose to use the existing surface and it has been painted with high-gloss paint, you will need to rough it up using sandpaper prior to your tile installation. Additionally, a setting material designed to bond to this surface, such as mastic, must be used. Be sure to plan ahead for any unique designs, such as recessed niches or ledges.

Floors If you are installing stone over a concrete slab, there are several things that must be done to ensure that the stone will bond properly and the installation will last. First, clean the slab to rid its surface of any excess dirt, paint, drywall mud, etc. If any visible cracks are evident, purchase a crack suppressant membrane and apply to those areas. This membrane is designed to expand with cracks appearing in the slab without breaking the tile. Check for high spots in the application area. This can be done using a 4-foot level or a long piece of rigid metal. A chalk line can also be used as a simple method of checking for consistency within the slab.

Begin by snapping lines from different angles within the room and then observing where the chalk line is lighter or nonexistent. Mark the high spots on the slab. If the high spots are severe the low areas of the floor will need to be filled or floated before the stone can be installed. Filling low spots with mortar and allowing them to cure before starting the installation is one option. A better choice is to use a self level-ing compound. Mixed properly, it will flow naturally into the low areas, resulting in a smooth, even surface. This leveling material is available at home centers and specialty tile stores. Be sure to recheck your area after the mortar or leveling compound has set. It is often wise to begin the installation at the highest area and allow for low spots by using additional mortar as needed.

If the floor is off grade, as with wooden decks, houses with crawl spaces, homes elevated on pilings, or upstairs flooring, the wood subflooring must be covered to create a rigid structure that is strong enough to support the tile and to provide the proper surface for an adequate tile bond.

Several options are available for subflooring. They include a variety of cement boards that are attached to the plywood base using an adhesive, a thin-set mortar, or screws. Synthetic materials are also available that provide not only structural stability, but act as a noise barrier as well. Consult your specialty tile dealer before proceeding with any other alternatives.

Shower Pans This is one area where you might want to consider soliciting help from a professional. The installation of the shower pan is complicated, but not impossible for the do-it-yourselfer. However, it is an area that if done incorrectly can result in future damages and drainage problems. Simply stated—it isn't worth taking the chance.

Shower Walls Shower walls should be clad with cement board in all areas receiving tile, including niches. The cement board should once again be screwed directly into the studs. If sheetrock or green board has been previously installed, it must be removed at least to the highest point where the tile extends. Shower seats can be constructed using pressure treated plywood and clad with cement board or be created from cinder block.

Tub Decks Clad all surface areas including the deck, splash area, and tub front with cement board. If this is a remodel and the tub and its housing structure already exist, make certain that there is enough play in the plumbing to accommodate the thickness of the cement board, mortar and tile before proceeding with your project.

TRICKS OF THE TRADE: INSTALLATION

Step One

Now that the prep work has been completed, let's get ready to lay the stone. One of the most important and frequently overlooked aspects of a natural stone installation is the separation of tiles with regard to color variation. Mother Nature added her artistic touch to stone by making the material unique, colorful, and inconsistent. Good professional installers are artists that make the stone flow throughout the application. Your job will reflect a more professional appearance if you take the time to divide the stone according to both color and characteristics and decide ahead of time how you want it to look when completed. Set aside tiles that exhibit unique and dramatic veining. Stone tiles that display extreme color variation can be either blended or used for focal points such as in borders, inserts, or artistic rug patterns. Stones with strong veining structures can be placed adjacent to each other resulting in a long continuous pattern that appears almost slablike.

In the case of slate and sandstone, the thickness of the tile itself can vary dramatically. It is more important than ever to divide these tiles into groupings of like thickness as well as color. These particular stones, especially when purchased ungauged, present the biggest challenge when it comes to laying a level floor. Begin with the thicker tiles and finish with the thinner. By using this process, additional mortar can be added to the thinner tiles, thereby resulting in a level installation.

Step Two

You must determine exactly where to begin the installation process. Whether the tile will be set horizontal or vertical, the first thing necessary to ascertain is the center point of the application. This is done by measuring, marking, and snapping chalk lines. Once you have established the center or starting point, dry fit the tiles to ensure that the measurements are accurate and that tiles of equal size border the perimeter. It is imperative that the first row of tiles be set straight. While the dry fit tiles are still in place, make any changes with regard to specific tiles and then as you pick them up, stack them conveniently and in the order that you wish to lay them.

Step Three

Once you have laid out your installation area and have a pretty good idea of what the finished project will look like, it is time to mix the setting compound. Most stone tiles are set using a product called thinset mortar. Because natural stone is extremely heavy, the consistency of the mortar should be firm enough to assure that the trowel ridges remain turgid and do not collapse under the weight of the tile. If the mortar is too wet, tiles will sink and will result in what is commonly referred to as lippage, or uneven tiles. If the mortar is too dry, it may fail to properly adhere to the tile, resulting in a faulty installation that will experience future problems. A quality grade thinset should always be used. Thinset mortar containing a latex additive will create a better, stronger bond than a general purpose one. Latex modified, or bonding mortars, should always be used for vertical wall applications or where frequent water exposure is likely.

When deciding on what color mortar to select, be sure to chose white for light colored stones, and the less expensive gray for the darker ones.

Stone tile should be back-buttered just prior to setting. This procedure will improve adhesion by ensuring that the entire tile is in contact with the setting material. The process of back-buttering is very simple. A thin layer of mortar is applied over the entire back side of the tile using the un-notched edge of your trowel or a margin trowel, in a manner reminiscent of buttering a piece of toast. This is a good time to add a little extra mortar where needed to keep the job level.

Remember that the smaller the grout joint between tiles, the more difficult they will be to level. Tiles that are butt jointed are the most difficult to install because there is little margin for error. In cases where the installer is not proficient, the job ends up with obvious lippage and raised edges. Although you can go back later and sand lippage on limestone and travertine tile with a belt sander, you will find this process leaves unattractive scratched looking areas where the sanding process took place. Professionals will go back over an uneven stone tile installation with a large machine that utilizes a wet sanding process, grinding the stone floor in place to a smooth flat finish. Once the floor is sanded to perfection, a process to bring the stone surface back up to its original honed or polished finish is begun. This procedure is definitely one best left to the pros.

When setting, gently press each tile into the thinset and use your fingertips to match it to the edges of the adjacent tile, feeling for any obvious high spots. Work the tile into the thinset. Keep your level handy to assure that the tiles are being set and kept level. You should expect to have to periodically pull up or lift a tile, possibly several times, to add or remove mortar, before it is set properly. Because the surface suction can be rather strong, it is advisable to use your margin trowel or, at the very least, a tool that won't flex when lifting ill-fitting tiles. Be prepared to break a few on occasion. When you're satisfied with the tile's placement, sponge away any surface mortar, as it may later interfere with the grout application. Also, when you reach your stopping point for the day, clean all tile edges of any excess mortar. If this mortar is allowed to set up, you will spend a good portion of your next day chiseling or grinding it away. Mortar should be allowed to set or dry for approximately twenty-four hours before being walked on so don't forget to rope off and clearly mark newly installed tiles.

Step Four

After all of the tiles have been set and the mortar has cured, a coat of penetrating sealer should be applied. It is important that the tiles be absolutely clean and dry before the application. The first coat of sealer, or a grout release, should be applied prior to grouting. This initial coat not only protects the stone from staining, but also makes grout cleanup much easier. Apply sealer with a small sprayer, sponge mop, or brush. Be sure to follow manufacturer's directions.

Step Five

The grout you select should complement the color of the stone, except in cases where the design stipulates otherwise. Sanded grout is used whenever grout lines are more than $\frac{1}{16}$-inch in width or in cases where large surface holes are being filled, as with unfilled travertine. Unsanded grout should be used with smaller grout joints, and with any stone prone to scratching. Grout should be mixed to the consistency of cake icing and applied using a grout float on a sponged damp tile. Remove excess grout from the tile surface immediately and recheck the surface as it dries, wiping away any haze as it forms. Grout that has been allowed to dry completely on surface areas will end up a cleaning nightmare. Buckets of clean, clear water should be readily available. To expedite the task of cleaning tile surfaces it is a good idea to use a two-bucket system, the grout-filled sponge can be rinsed first in one bucket and then rinsed again in the second bucket. Changing the water frequently is advisable and will ultimately facilitate the cleanup effort. Resist the temptation to over-wipe the grout. With a clean, only slightly damp sponge, make one pass, flip the sponge and make the second pass, then rinse the sponge. Any more wiping on the same spot only serves to spread the grout haze. Using a sponge that is too wet may cause efflorescence, or grout discoloration. Grout should be allowed to cure for the manufac-turer's recommended period, approximately forty-eight hours, before being sealed.

Step Six

After the grout has cured, sponge clean the floor once again and allow it to dry. Apply a second coat of penetrating sealer to both the grout and stone, possibly even a third. There are many excellent sealers on the market today that are guaranteed for up to twenty-five years, but use good judg-ment, more frequent applications may be needed depending on the amount of foot traffic and exposure to water and sunlight.

CARE AND MAINTENANCE

Caring for natural stone is not unlike car-ing for any other material in your home. If you maintain it properly, it will reward you for many years to come. Use common sense and the following tips to keep your installation attractive.

Countertops

Once your countertop has been correctly sealed, you shouldn't have to worry about staining, however, take precautions with anything acidic, such as alcohol, soda, coffee, and juice, and wipe spills quickly. Using cutting boards and coasters are not always priority, but will keep your coun-tertops looking new for much longer. As with floors, there are plenty of specialty cleaners on the market for cleaning your countertops. Be sure never to use acidic cleaners or vinegar when cleaning stone. Use only neutral pH substances.

Floors

As noted in earlier chapters, the best way to keep your stone floor in good condition is to keep it as free of dirt particles as pos-sible. The mix of foot traffic and grit will eventually cause the stone's surface to dull due to scratching. Prevent this from occur-ring by placing large quality floor mats outside each entryway. In addition to reducing the amount of dirt that makes its way in, keep it to a minimum by sweeping routinely with a clean, nontreated dry dust mop. You can also simply vacuum. Just be sure that the bottom of your vacuum cleaner is in good repair, to prevent any scratching.

Periodically you will want to mop your stone floor to keep it looking new. There are plenty of specialty cleaners on the market made specifically for cleaning natural stone. They are affordable and easy to use. You may also consider a steamer vac on your stone floor. To be safe, check with your stone dealer as to the appropriateness of use on your specific stone type.

Ongoing maintenance and repair

Unless you have installed a polished stone other than granite on the countertop or floor, you will not experience the need for future repairs very often. Most polished stones will need to be professionally resurfaced on occasion to restore their original shine. Slate, limestone, travertine, granite, and aged stone will all age wonderfully with use. There may be a possibility that a tile or two may crack over time due to a variety of reasons. A repair of this type is fairly inexpensive and easy to do if you have pieces of the original tile on hand. You may need to apply additional penetrating sealer to your stone every few years or as needed. A limestone or travertine countertop may need etch marks or water rings removed periodically; this is not usually a major expense and can often be taken on by the experienced do-it-your-selfer.

Overall, natural stone is not a material that requires a lot of upkeep to continue looking good. It truly is one of the few building materials that ages gracefully.

COST FACTORS: STONE VS MAN-MADE

Stone has long been associated with wealth and prestige. Until recently, it was a material used for primarily high-end commercial and residential projects only. With advances in technology and a greater supply to meet the demand, natural stone has become affordable to most homeowners. Whether you are building a brand new home or just spicing up your current abode, the following table will help you get an idea of costs associated with stone versus man-made materials.

There are many factors that can affect the cost of stone. Some showrooms buy in bulk or from a direct importer and pass their savings along to the consumer. Some retailers buy from a middleman; therefore a higher mark up is necessary. In addition, there are materials that are just pricier than others for a variety of reasons. Some stone types may be readily available and some may be rare and exotic. You may find a deeply discounted stone, but buyer beware, there is probably a good reason for it.

In regard to a stone slab, the cost is reflected primarily in the labor of fabrication. The thickness will cause the price to fluctuate, as does the number of cutouts employed and the choice of edge profile.

Because of the significant variations in cost, ranges are notes in place of an exact price. It is wise to do your research; you may find that stone you love for a substantially lower price.

STONE	SLAB (Installed)	TILE (Material only)
Granite	$$$$ to $$$$$	$$$
Marble	$$$$ to $$$$$	$$$
Limestone	$$$$	$$ to $$$
Travertine	$$$$	$ to $$
Slate	$$$$	$
Soapstone	$$$$	$$
Antiquated Stone	$$$$ to $$$$$	$$$ to $$$$
Solid Surface (Corian)	$$$$ to $$$$$	N/A
Laminate	$$$ to $$$$	N/A
Stainless Steel	$$$$ to $$$$$	N/A
Ceramic	N/A	$ to $$$$

KEY

$: 2 to 4 dollars per square foot

$$: 5 to 9 dollars per square foot

$$$: 10 to 19 dollars per square foot

$$$$: 20 to 40 dollars per square foot

$$$$$: 41 dollars per square foot and up

GLOSSARY

Acid washed: Stone treated with acidic substances to accelerate the aging process.

Adoquin: A stone quarried in Mexico composed primarily of quartz based minerals and volcanic rock.

Ashlar Pattern: A random setting pattern using various sizes of square and rectangular tile. The effect is old-world style.

Back-buttering: The process of slathering the back of a stone tile with thinset material in order to ensure proper mortar coverage. This prevents hollow areas and subsequent future cracking of tiles. Also helpful to insure a level installation.

Backsplash: The area located between the countertop and lower cabinet. Normally 16–18 inches in height.

Bluestone: A hard metamorphic sandstone quarried in the United States. Commonly found in shades of blue, violet, and buff.

Brick pattern: The method of setting rectangular tiles in a staggered or offset fashion, thus creating the look of brick.

Brushed finish: A finish obtained by brushing the stone's surface with a coarse wire rotary brush. Surfaces may take on a leathery appearance.

Border: A decorative piece of tile, often long and narrow, set within the field tiles to create interest.

Bullnose: Rounding of an exposed stone edge.

Bush hammered: A mechanical process of beating the stone surface to give it a subtle or dramatic texture.

Calibrated tile: When a stone tile has been machine cut on both sides, offering a like thickness, it has been calibrated.

Cantera stone: Similar to adoquin stone, but not as dense. Quarried in Mexico.

Chamfer: A beveled tile edge can also be referred to as a chamfered edge.

Checkerboard pattern: Alternating square tiles of differing colors or shades creates a checkerboard effect.

Chiseled edge: A process of mechanically chipping the tile edge, thus giving the stone a rustic, aged appearance.

Cladding: When a wall is faced in a stone it can be referred to as clad.

Cleavage: The natural splitting point of a stone mass.

Cleft finish: When the surface of a stone is rough, due to the quarry method of splitting the material along its natural plane, it is referred to as a cleft finish or surface. Normally associated with slate.

Cobblestone: A stone that has the appearance of being naturally rounded or distressed, due to many years of use or weathering.

Coquina: A limestone primarily extracted in Florida, comprised of seashells and calcite.

Cross-cut: The process of cutting the initial block of stone parallel to the natural bedding plane. The effect is a mottled or cloudlike appearance.

Cure time: The time required for the thinset below the tile to become hard and set.

Eased edge: When referring to a slab material, the square edge profile normally has softened edges as opposed to sharp square edges for added safety.

Efflorescence: The appearance of a white powderlike substance on the stone's surface or grout, which is often the result of the accumulation of salts due to excessive moisture.

Etched: A decorative surface pattern created by a variety of methods, most often with abrasive chemicals or sandblasting.

Face: The portion of the stone tile or slab that is exposed.

Field stone: A stone found above ground, normally worn and weathered.

Filled Stone: When a stone's open pores have been prefilled with a stone dust resin or epoxy at the factory, this is referred to as filled. Commonly associated with travertine.

Forty-five: Another way of describing diagonal setting patterns.

Flagstone: Thick flat pieces of stone in various shapes used to pave walkways, driveways, or patios.

Flamed finish: A very rough textured surface achieved through direct exposure to intense heat and flame. Normally associated with granite.

Fleuri cut: The process of cutting the stone parallel to the bedding plane. The effect is a cloudlike or mottled appearance.

Gang saw: The large wet saw that cuts raw blocks of stone down into a specified thickness.

Gauged stone: Machine grinding stone tiles to ensure a uniform thickness is referred to as gauging.

Granite: A hard, crystalline, igneous rock formation formed from extreme heat, comprised of various minerals such as feldspar and quartz.

Grout: A cementous or epoxy based material used to fill joints between tiles. Available in a large range of colors.

Guillotine cut: Cutting a stone tile, most often slate, by the guillotine method offers a ragged and chipped edge.

Herringbone pattern: A method of setting rectangular tiles slanted, creating a zigzag effect.

Honed finish: A satin smooth finish. It exhibits a flat or matte appearance, as opposed to the reflective glasslike finish of a polished stone.

Igneous: A type of rock formed from the cooling and solidification of molten matter.

Inserts: Decorative tiles or accents can be inserted into the area where four field tiles meet, or creatively placed in the center of a stone tile.

Joint: The area where two tiles or two slabs meet.

Limestone: A rock formed from the sedimentary process, underground and underwater, comprised primarily of calcium deposits of shell and bone.

Liner: A long narrow piece of decorative tile placed within a field of stone to add interest or break up a pattern.

Lippage: The joints where the tiles meet are differing in height, in reference to tile floors or walls. Industry standards allow for $\frac{1}{16}$-inch height variance between tiles.

Marble: A limestone capable of receiving a high polished finish.

Metamorphic rock: A type of rock altered in appearance by intense pressure, heat, or a combination of both.

Mortar: The material used to set stone tile. Composed of water, cement, sand, and lime.

Mosaic: A field of tiles created from numerous small irregular shaped pieces. Often set in a way to depict a pattern or picture.

Ninety: When placing a tile perpendicular to the wall or in a square fashion, it may be referred to as on the ninety.

Onyx: A banded, translucent form of marble, found in caves.

Pallet: Stone tiles are normally crated and shipped from abroad on a strong wooden frame referred to as a pallet.

Parquetry: An inlaid floor consisting of geometric shapes and two or more stone types or colors.

Patina: When the surface of a material has changed in color or texture due to age or exposure to various elements, it is referred to as patina.

Pillowed: A tile finish that features softly rounded edges, thus giving the tile a pillowed look.

Polished finish: A shiny, high-gloss finish, normally attained on very hard stones. This finish draws out the deepest color and full character of the stone.

Quarry: A physical location where raw blocks of stone or other stone deposits are removed from the earth.

Quartzite: A stone composed of primarily the mineral quartz and sandstone.

Rug pattern: An inlaid floor design comprised of various materials, patterned to resemble a throw rug placed on the floor.

Sandblasted: A rough surface texture achieved through a high-pressure blast of sand.

Sandstone: A rock formed from the sedimentary process consisting primarily of quartz cemented together by calcium carbonate or silica.

Saw cut: A rough surface finish, often exposing saw marks from the stone's initial cutting. It is highly slip resistant, and offers a more rustic appearance than a honed or polished stone.

Serpentine: A marble composed primarily of the mineral serpentine.

Slab: A linear piece of stone cut from the original quarried block.

Slate: A rock composed of shale and clay.

Soapstone: A form of rock composed of the minerals steatite and talc.

Split face: A finish that exhibits a rough chiseled face, similar to a raw block of stone fresh from the quarry.

Tile mural: A painting or picture projected onto a field of stones. Used for decoration.

Travertine: A form of rock created from limestone, but near hot bubbling springs, thus creating its inherent pitted surface.

Tumbled: An aged finish achieved by placing stone in a tumbling machine or drum, occasionally with the addition of acids or other materials to soften the stone edges and give the surface a worn effect.

Undulated: A surface finish that is wavy, giving the stone the appearance of thousands of years of foot traffic.

Unfilled: When a stone has pits and holes upon its surface that have not been filled with stone dust resin or epoxy at the factory, it is referred to as unfilled. Commonly associated with travertine.

Un-gauged: When a tile has been cut with out strict adherence to uniform thickness, it is referred to as ungauged.

Vein cut: The process of cutting the initial block of stone perpendicular to the natural bedding plane. Enhances the horizontal vein structure.

Weathering: Aging of a surface through the effects of weather.

DIRECTORY OF RESOURCES

ARCHITECTS, DESIGNERS, and BUILDERS

Benning Design Associates
1707 18th Street
Sacramento, CA 95814
Tel (916) 448-8120
Fax (916) 444-9275
www.benningdesign.com
Email@benningdesign.com

Bruce Bierman Design, Inc.
29 West 15th Street
New York, NY 10011
Tel (212) 243-1935
Fax (212) 243-6615
www.biermandesign.com
Info@biermandesign.com

DCSW Architects
Jeffery J. Seres AIA
130 Grant Avenue Suite 102
Santa Fe, NM 87501
Tel (505) 982-7191
Fax (505) 992-0585
www.dcswarchitects.com

de Giulio kitchen design
674 North Wells Street
Chicago, IL 60610
Tel (847) 256-8833
Fax (847) 256-8842
www.degiulio.org
Info@degiulio.org

Dorado Designs
4640 E. Sunrise Drive
Suite 118
Tucson, AZ 85718
Tel (520) 577-1800
Fax (520) 577-7916
www.doradodesigns.com
Info@doradodesigns.com

London Bay Homes
9130 Galleria Court
Suite 200
Naples, FL 34109
Tel (239) 592-1400
www.londonbay.com

Marc-Michaels Interior Design Inc.
720 West Morse Boulevard
Winter Park, FL 32789
Tel (407) 629-2124
Fax (407) 629-9437
www.marc-michaels.com
Info@marc-michaels.com

Mikal L. Otten CKD
115 Madison Street
Denver, CO 80206
Tel (303) 321-3232
Fax (303) 321-8299
Motten@wmohs.com

Liz Ryan Interior Design
6262 N. Swan Road
Suite 185
Tucson, AZ 85718
Tel (520) 299-2123
Fax (520) 299-2134
www.lizryandesign.com
Liz@lizryandesign.com

Lori Carroll and Associates
1200 N. El Dorado Place
Suite B-200
Tucson, AZ 85715
Tel (520) 886-3443
Fax (520) 886-1768
www.loricarroll.com
Lori@loricarroll.com

Jackie Naylor Interiors
4287 Glengary Drive N.E.
Atlanta, GA 30342
Tel (404) 814-1973
Fax (404) 814-9030

Shamir Shah Design
10 Greene Street
New York, NY 10013
Tel (212) 274-7476
Fax (212) 274-7477

Sidnam, Petrone, and Gartner
136 West 21st Street
New York, NY 10011
Tel (212) 366-5500
Fax (212) 366-6559
www.spgarchitects.com
Info@spgarchitects.com

DESIGNER SHOWROOMS

Ann Sacks Tile & Stone
8120 N.E. 33rd Drive
Portland, OR 97211
Tel (800) 278-8453
www.annsacks.com

Country Floors Australia
2 Aquatic Drive
French Forest NSW 2086
Australia
Tel (011-612) 9453 9466
Fax (011-612) 9453 9828
www.countryfloors.com.au
Info@countryfloors.com.au

Dal Tile
7834 CF Hawn Fwy
Dallas, TX 75217
Tel (214) 398-1411
www.daltile.com

Downsview Kitchens
2635 Rena Road
Mississauga, Ontario, Canada
L4T-1G6
Tel (905) 677-9354
Fax (905) 677-5776
www.downsviewkitchens.com

Haifa Inc.
2949 2nd Avenue North
Lake Worth, FL 33461
Tel (561) 641-4911
Fax (561) 641-8763
www.haifainc.com
Info@haifainc.com

Materials Marketing
1234 West Fulton Street
Chicago, IL 60607
Tel (312) 226-0222
Fax (312) 226-3790
www.materials-marketing.com

Mystic Marble & Granite
100 West Colonial Drive
Orlando, FL 32801
Tel (407) 872-7717
Fax (407) 872-7750
www.mysticgranite.com
web designer: Hillary Kendrick of
Image Architects

Natural Stone Design LLC
35-B Gulf Breeze Parkway
Gulf Breeze, FL 32561
Tel (850) 916-9767
www.naturalstonedesign.com
Dnaturalstone@aol.com

Paris Ceramics
583 Kings Road
London SW6 2EH
Tel ++ 44(0) 20 7371-7778
www.parisceramics.com
London@parisceramics.com

Rutt of Atlanta
351 Peachtree Hills Avenue N.E.
Suite 413
Atlanta, GA 30305
Tel (404) 264-9698
www.rutt1.com
Showroom@ruttatlanta.com

Walker Zanger
8901 Bradley Avenue
Sun Valley, CA 91352
Tel (818) 504-0235
Fax (818) 504-2057
www.walkerzanger.com

William Ohs Timeless Handmade Cabinetry
115 Madison Street
Denver, CO 80206
Tel (303) 321-3232
Fax (303) 321-8299
www.wmohs.com

ARTISTS and MANUFACTURERS

Ancient Venetian Floor Company
1516 Edison Street
Dallas, TX 75207
Tel (214) 741-4555
Fax (214) 741-4147
www.ancientvenetianfloor.com

Antiquestone
P.O. Box 434
Bertram, TX 78605
Tel (512) 355-2722
Fax (512) 355-2752
www.antiquestone.com

Architerra
1701 Evergreen Suite 2
Austin, TX 78704
Tel (512) 441-8062
www.architerra.com

Artistic Stone
P.O. Box 237
Hunters Hill NSW 2110
Australia
Tel ++ 02-9712-2444
Fax ++ 02-9712-5109
www.artisticstone.com.au

Artsaics
1006 Grand Boulevard
Deer Park, NY 11729
Tel (631) 254-2558
Fax (631) 254-2451
www.artsaics.com

Barbara Tattersfield
425 W. New England Avenue
Suite 200
Winter Park, FL 32789
Tel (407) 644-1500
Fax (407) 644-8331
www.stone-50.com
Info@stone-50.com

Bordofino
7957 N.W. 54th Street
Miami, FL 33166
Tel (305) 471-0213
Fax (305) 471-0691
www.bordofino.com
Bordofino@aol.

Bronzework Studio
4401 N. Ravenswood Avenue
Chicago, IL 60640
Tel (773) 784-2628
www.bronzeworkstudio.com
Bronzeworkstudio@lowitzandcompany.com

Foundry Art Fine Bronze
4401 N. Ravenswood Avenue
Chicago, IL 60640
Tel (773) 784-2628
www.foundryartbronze.com
foundryart@lowitzandcompany.com

Intarsia
9550 Satellite Boulevard, Suite 180
Orlando, FL 32837
Tel (407) 859-5800
Fax (407) 859-7555
www.intarsiainc.com

Mesa Precast Supply, Inc.
808 S. McClintock Drive
Tempe, AZ 85281
Tel (480) 968-5400
Fax (480) 894-0375
www.mesaprecast.com

Oceanside Glasstile
2293 Cosmos Court
Carlsbad, CA 92009
Tel (760) 929-4082
Fax (760) 929-5882
www.glasstile.com

Sonoma Tile Makers
7750 Bell Road
Windsor, CA 95492
www.sonomatilemakers.com

**The Thierry Francois Collection
from Stone Age Designs**
351 Peachtree Hills Avenue N.E., Suite 501A
Atlanta, GA 30305
Tel (404) 350-3333
Fax (404) 842-0936
www.stoneagedesigns.net

Ron Goeke Studio
Tel (609) 597-4880
Fax (609) 597-0865
www.rgstudio.net

Sienna Marble and Mosaic
3963 Domestic Avenue
Naples, FL 34104
Tel (941) 435-7875
Fax (941) 435-9942
www.siennamarble.com

Studio Vertu
1208 Central Parkway
Cincinnati, OH 45210
Tel (513) 241-9038
Fax (513) 241-0057
www.studiovertu.com

Talisman Handmade Stoneware Tiles
4401 N. Ravenswood Avenue
Chicago, IL 60640
Tel (773) 784-2628
www.talismantile.com
Talisman@lowitzandcompany.com

IMPORTERS, DISTRIBUTORS, and FABRICATORS

AKDO Intertrade
675 East Washington Avenue
Bridgeport, CT 06608
Tel (203) 336-5199
Fax (203) 336-0603
www.akdointertrade.com

American Slate Group
835 McEntyre Lane
Decatur, AL 35601
Tel (256) 350-9888
Fax (256) 350-2856
www.americanslategroup.com

Granite-Tops Inc.
12384 234th Street
Cold Spring, MN 56320
Tel (320) 685-3005
Fax (320) 685-3006
www.granite-topsinc.com

Keys Granite
8788 NW 27th Street
Miami, FL 33122
Tel (305) 477-7363
Fax (305) 471-8199
www.keysgranite.com

Mureks International
4900 Rio Vista Avenue
Tampa, FL 33634
Tel (813) 249-5800
www.mureks.com
Info@mureks.com

Stockett Tile & Granite Co.
7329 E. Greenway Road
Scottsdale, AZ 85260
Tel (480) 443-1988
Fax (480) 596-9672
www.stockett.com

Tureks
2737 Dorr Avenue
Fairfax, VA 22031
Tel (703) 204-1818
Fax (703) 204-1888
www.tureks.com.tr
Info@marblesystems.com

STONE CARE PRODUCTS AND EQUIPMENT

Alpha Professional Tools
250 Braen Avenue
Wyckoff, NJ 07481
Tel (201) 447-4330
Fax (201) 447-1128
www.alpha-tools.com

Aqua Mix
10400 Pioneer Boulevard
Suite 8
Santa Fe Springs, CA 90670
Tel (562) 946-8877
Fax (562) 903- 1963
www.aquamix.com

Braxton Bragg Corp.
6031 Tazewell Pike
Knoxville, TN 37918
Tel 1 (800) 575-4401
Fax 1 (800) 915-5501
www.braxtonbragg.com

HMK Stone Care
1555 Burke Avenue, Suite C
San Francisco, CA 94124
Tel (415) 643-5603
Fax (415) 643-5647
www.hmkstonecare.com

Miracle Sealants Company
12318 Lower Azusa Road
Arcadia, CA 91006
Tel (626) 443-6433
Fax (626) 443-1435
www.miraclesealants.com

Plasplugs Portable Wet Saw
www.plasplugs.com

Stone Care International
3681 Ashley Way
Owings Mills, MD 21117
Tel (410) 783-0045
Fax (410) 783-1625
www.stonecare.com

Tile Lab
13001 Seal Beach Boulevard
Seal Beach, CA 90740
Tel (562) 598-8808
Fax (562) 598-4008
www.tilelab.com

NATIONAL ORGANIZATIONS

American Institute of Architects
www.aia.org

American Society of Interior Designers
www.asid.org

Marble Institute of America
www.marble-institute.com

National Homebuilders of America
www.nahb.com

National Kitchen and Bath Association
www.nkba.com

National Training Institute for Stone and
Masonry Trades www.ntc-stone.com

WEBSITES

www.natural-stone.com

www.findstone.com

www.stoneinfo.com

www.StoneExpoZone.com

www.naturalstonedesign.com

PHOTOGRAPHERS

Antoine Bootz
123 West 20th Street, # 2B
New York, NY 10011
Tel (212) 366-9041
Fax (212) 366- 9386

Stephen Dabrowski
10806 Overland Avenue
Culver City, CA 90230
Tel (310) 559-7211

Brett Drury ASMP
Specializing in Architectural Photography
3165 Bernardo Lane
Escondido, CA 92029
Tel (760) PHOTO-US
www.architectural-photography.com
Bdrury@architectural-photography.com

David Duncan Livingston
1036 Erica Road
Mill Valley, CA 94941
Tel (415) 305-6050
Fax (415) 383-0897
www.davidduncanlivingston.com

Ken Nelson Photography
P.O. Box 32725
Palm Beach Gardens, FL 33420
Tel (561) 373-5371
www.kennelsonphotography.com
Ken@kennelsonphotography.com

Michael Dunne
54 Stokenchurch Street
London SW63TR
Tel ++44(0) 20-7736-6171
Fax ++44(0) 20-7731-8792
Michael@dunne.dircon.co.uk

Mimi Pfeil
514 Golf Course Road
Winder, GA 30680
Tel (770) 867-7989

James Yochum Photography
12330 Betty May Street
Sawyer, MI 49125
Tel (616) 426-8484
Fax (616) 426-8485
www.jamesyochum.com

John Umberger
Real Images
340 Outback Ridge Trail
Jasper, GA 30143
Tel (678) 290-7800

Kim Sargent
7675 Steeplechase Drive
Palm Beach Gardens, FL 33418
Tel (561) 881-8887
Fax (561) 881-8882
www.sargentphoto.com

Lawrence Taylor Architectural Photography
2000-B Alden Road
Orlando, FL 32803
Tel (407) 897-2005
Fax (407) 897-2252

Matthew Millman Photography
821 Richmond Street
El Cerrito, CA 94530
Tel (510) 459-9030
Fax (510) 526-1778

Pieter Estersohn
26 Gramercy Park South
Penthouse North
New York, NY 10003
Tel (212) 979-1212
Fax (212) 979-9605
www.pieterestersohn.com

Richard L. Faller Photography
825 Early Street, #E-11
Santa Fe, NM 87505
Tel (505) 982-5846

Robert Thien
2432 Sunrise Drive
Atlanta, GA 30345
Tel (404) 486-9813

Tim Street-Porter
2074 Watsonia Terrace
Hollywood, CA 90068
Tel (323) 874-4278
Fax (323) 876-8795

FLOOR PLAN DIAGRAMS:
RANDOM PATTERN LAYOUTS

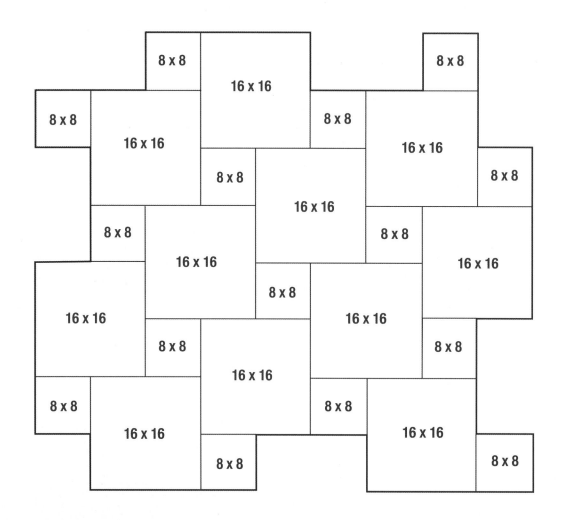

**This plan can be modified to range from 6 x 6 to 12 x 12
All measurements are in inches

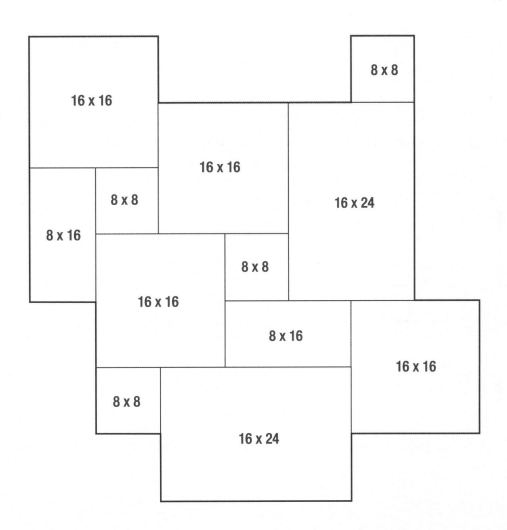

6 x 6	6 x 16	6 x 6	6 x 16	6 x 6	6 x 16	6 x 6
6 x 16	16 x 16	6 x 16	16 x 16	6 x 16	16 x 16	6 x 16
6 x 6	6 x 16	6 x 6	6 x 16	6 x 6	6 x 16	6 x 6
6 x 16	16 x 16	6 x 16	16 x 16	6 x 16	16 x 16	6 x 16
6 x 16	16 x 16	6 x 16	16 x 16	6 x 16	16 x 16	6 x 16

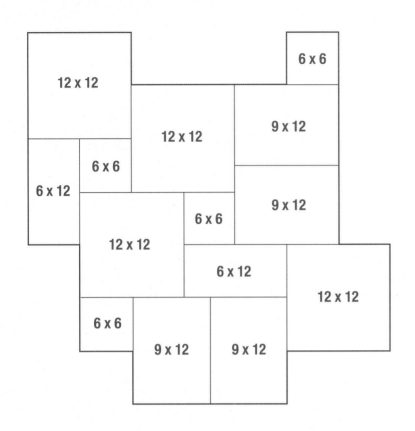

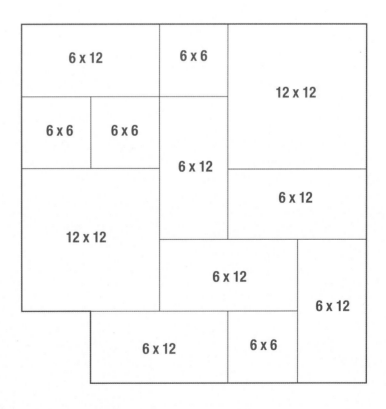

PHOTO CREDITS

Page 1: Photo courtesy of Kim Sargent
Page 2: Talisman Tiles/Ann Sacks
Page 6 top to bottom: Country Floors Australia/Designer Victoria Murray; Country Floors Australia/Designer Victoria Murray; Paris Ceramics
Page 7 top to bottom: Photo by Stephen Dabrowski/Barbara Tattersfield Design; Ann Sacks
Page 9: Photo © Pieter Estersohn
Page 10 left to right: Sonoma Tile Makers; Dal-Tile; Paris Ceramics
Page 13: Photo courtesy of Kim Sargent
Page 14 top to bottom: Country Floors Australia/Designer Victoria Murray; Bottom Left to Right; © davidduncanlivingston.com; © davidduncanlivingston.com; Ann Sacks
Page 16 top to bottom: © davidduncanlivingston.com; Tim Street-Porter/ Beateworks.com
Page 17: Photo courtesy of Kim Sargent/ Interior design by Marc-Michaels Interior Design, Inc.
Page 18 Tile 1: Granite-Tops, Inc.; Tile 2: Mystic Marble and Granite/Hillary Kendricks; Tile 3, 4, 5: Dal-Tile
Pages 18–19: Photo courtesy of deGulio Kitchen Design, Inc.
Page 19: Photo © Walker Zanger, Inc.
Page 20: © 1998–2002 Laurence Taylor. Photo courtesy of London Bay Homes
Page 21: Courtesy of Downsview Kitchens
Page 22 left to right: © davidduncanlivingston.com; Hoyle/Beateworks.com
Page 23: Photo by Ray Albright/Design by Dorado Designs
Page 24: © davidduncanlivingston.com
Page 25: Ann Sacks
Page 26: Caillaut/Beateworks.com
Page 27: Hoyle/Beateworks.com
Page 28 top to bottom: Photo © Artsaics Studio; Photo © Artsaics Studio; Photo © Artsaics Studio; Studio Vertu; Studio Vertu

Pages 28–29: Photo courtesy of Kim Sargent
Page 30 left to right: Wauman/ Beateworks.com; Stockett Tile & Granite Co.
Page 31: Dal-Tile
Page 32: Materials Marketing
Page 33: Courtesy of Downsview Kitchens
Page 34: © davidduncanlivingston.com
Page 35: Image © James Yochum Photography/Design by Dorado Designs
Page 36: Courtesy of Haifa, Inc.
Page 37: Courtesy of Downsview Kitchens
Page 38: Mystic Marble and Granite/Hillary Kendricks
Page 39: Courtesy of Downsview Kitchens
Pages 40–41: © davidduncanlivingston.com
Page 41 top to bottom: Photo © Walker Zanger, Inc.; Ann Sacks; Photo © Walker Zanger, Inc.
Page 42: © davidduncanlivingston.com
Page 43: Photo © Walker Zanger, Inc.
Page 44: Photo © Artsaics Studio
Page 45 top to bottom: Studio Vertu; © davidduncanlivingston.com
Page 46: Saharoff/Beateworks.com
Page 47 top to bottom: Studio Vertu; © davidduncanlivingston.com
Page 48: Photo by Manfred Studios/ Courtesy of Foundry Art and Ann Sacks
Page 49: Courtesy of The Place for Tile, Inc./Bordofino
Page 50: Photo courtesy of Materials Marketing
Page 51: Photo © Brett Drury
Page 52: Photo by Ray Albright/Design by Dorado Designs
Page 53: © 1998–2002 Laurence Taylor. Photo courtesy of London Bay Homes
Page 54: The Thierry François Collection available at Stone Age Designs
Page 55: © 1998–2002 Laurence Taylor. Photo courtesy of London Bay Homes
Page 56: Photo courtesy of Materials Marketing
Page 57: Courtesy of Haifa, Inc.

Page 58 top: Country Floors Australia/Design by Victoria Murray; bottom left to right: Photo by Christopher Ray/Courtesy of Oceanside Glasstile; Country Floors Australia; Country Floors Australia/Design by Victoria Murray
Page 60: Country Floors Australia
Pages 60–61: Tim Street-Porter/ Beateworks.com
Page 61: Dook/Beateworks.com
Page 62–63: Tim Street-Porter/ Beatworks.com
Page 64: Murals; Studio Vertu; © davidduncanlivingston.com
Page 65: Photo by Mark Mills/courtesy of Oceanside Glass Tile
Page 66 left to right: Country Floors Australia/Design by Victoria Murray; Ann Sacks
Page 67 left to right: © davidduncanlivingston.com; Photo © Walker Zanger, Inc.
Page 68: © davidduncanlivingston.com
Pages 68–69: Photo by John Umberger, Real Images/Design by Michelle Rosenberg, James Wade/courtesy of Rutt of Atlanta
Page 69: Ann Sacks
Page 70: © davidduncanlivingston.com
Page 71 top left: Photo © Pieter Estersohn; top right: © davidduncanlivingston.com; bottom: Photo by Michael Dunne/Design by Bruce Bierman
Page 72 left to right: Photo by Christopher Ray/courtesy of Oceanside Glasstile; © davidduncanlivingston.com
Page 73: Country Floors Australia/Design by Victoria Murray
Page 74 top: Stockett Tile & Granite Co.; left to right: photo by Mimi Pfeil; photo by Matthew Millman/Design by Dorado Designs
Page 75: Paris Ceramics
Page 76: © 1998–2002 Laurence Taylor. Photo courtesy of London Bay Homes
Page 77: Bill Geddes/Beateworks.com

Page 78 left to right: Liz Ryan Interior Design; Photo by Robert Thien/Design by Jackie Naylor Interiors

Page 79 left to right: Ann Sacks; photo courtesy of Kim Sargent

Page 80: Photo by Matthew Millman/Design by Dorado Designs

Page 81: Ann Sacks

Page 82 top: Paris Ceramics; bottom left to right: Photo © Pieter Estersohn; © david-duncanlivingston.com; Photo by Brett Drury

Page 84 left: Country Floors Australia; right top to bottom: Ann Sacks; photo © Walker Zanger, Inc.

Page 85: Paris Ceramics

Page 86: Courtesy of Ancient Venetian Floor Company

Page 87: © davidduncanlivingston.com

Page 88: Photo © Pieter Estersohn

Page 89 left: Photo by Ken Nelson/courtesy of Haifa, Inc.; right top to bottom: Foundry Art/Ann Sacks; photo © Walker Zanger, Inc.

Page 90: Paris Ceramics

Pages 90–91: Paris Ceramics

Page 91: Paris Ceramics

Page 92: Photo © Pieter Estersohn

Page 93: Foundry Art/Ann Sacks

Page 94 top and bottom: Photo © Walker Zanger, Inc.

Page 95 top left to right: Ann Sacks; © davidduncanlivingston.com; bottom left to right: Paris Ceramics; Paris Ceramics

Page 96: Photo © Pieter Estersohn

Page 97: Ann Sacks

Page 98 top to bottom: Tim Street-Porter/Beateworks.com; courtesy of Haifa, Inc.

Page 99: Photo by Ken Nelson/courtesy of Haifa, Inc.

Page 100 left to right: Country Floors Australia; photo © Walker Zanger, Inc.

Page 101: Photo by Richard Faller/DCSW Architects/Jeffery J. Seres AIA

Page 102 top: Photo by Stephen Dabrowski/Barbara Tattersfield Designs; bottom left to right: Photo courtesy Materials Marketing; Photo by Christopher Ray/Oceanside Glasstile; photo © 1998–2002 Laurence Taylor. Photo courtesy of London Bay Homes

Page 104: Tim Street-Porter/Beatworks.com

Page 105 top left to right: Photo © Walker Zanger, Inc.; Sonoma Tile Makers; bottom: photo courtesy of Kim Sargent

Page 106: © davidduncanlivingston.com

Page 107: © 1998–2002 Laurence Taylor. Photo courtesy of London Bay Homes

Page 108 left to right: The Thierry Francois Collection available at Stone Age Designs; photo courtesy of Kim Sargent/Interior design by Marc-Michaels Interior Design, Inc.

Page 109: Photo courtesy by Kim Sargent/Interior design by Marc-Michaels Interior Design, Inc.

Page 110: © 1998–2002 Laurence Taylor. Photo courtesy of London Bay Homes

Page 111: Photo courtesy of Kim Sargent/Interior design by Marc-Michaels Interior Design, Inc.

Page 112: © 1998–2002 Laurence Taylor. Photo courtesy of London Bay Homes

Page 113: Photo courtesy of Kim Sargent/Interior design by Marc-Michaels Interior Design, Inc.

Page 114 left to right: Wauman/Beateworks.com; Photo by Brett Drury

Page 115: Photo courtesy of Kim Sargent/Interior design by Marc-Michaels Interior Design, Inc.

Page 116 top to bottom: Materials Marketing; Photo by Stephen Dabrowski/Design by Barbara Tattersfield Designs

Page 117: © 1998–2002 Laurence Taylor.

photo courtesy of London Bay Homes

Page 118 left to right: Studio Vertu; photo courtesy of Kim Sargent

Page 119: Courtesy of Haifa, Inc.

Page 120 left to right: Materials Marketing; Photo courtesy of Kim Sargent

Page 121 left to right: © davidduncanlivingston.com; Studio Vertu

Page 122 top to bottom: Photo © Walker Zanger, Inc.; Studio Vertu

Page 123: Photo © Walker Zanger, Inc.

Page 124 top to bottom: Courtesy of Haifa, Inc.; Studio Vertu

Pages 124–125: Photo by Ray Albright/Design by Dorado Designs

Page 125: Hoyle/Beateworks.com

Page 126: Courtesy of Downsview Kitchens

Page 129 top: Ann Sacks; bottom left to right: photo by Heather Adams/product supplied by Architerra; Ancient Venetian Floor Company; Dal-Tile

Pages 131–139: Images provided by Granite-Tops, Inc.

Pages 140–143: Mystic Marble and Granite/Hillary Kendricks; photography © Walker Zanger, Inc.

Pages 144–145: Mystic Marble and Granite/Hillary Kendricks; Dal-Tile

Pages 146–147: Dal-Tile; photography © Walker Zanger, Inc.

Pages 148–149: Dal-Tile; Granite-Tops, Inc.

Page 150 sidebar: Artistic Stone Australia; top middle: photo © Artsaics Studio; bottom left to right: courtesy of Ancient Venetian Floor Company; photo © Artsaics Studio

Page 151 sidebar: Artistic Stone Australia; bottom: photo © Artsaics Studio

Page 152: Photo © Walker Zanger, Inc.

Page 153: Photo © Walker Zanger, Inc.

Page 154: Photo by Heather Adams/product supplied by Siena Marble and Granite

Page 192: Ann Sacks

INDEX

LIVING WITH STONE
A LIFETIME OF ENJOYMENT

If natural stone came with a label attached, it would read—I am a natural material. I am an individual unlike any other. Color and texture variations are inherent and make me beautiful. Imperfections are not defects but part of my charm. Take good care of me and I will reward you with a lifetime of beauty.

Don't let anyone talk you out of your dreams, pave the way to them with stone.